Praise for *Engaging Stude*

In *Engaging Students*, Phillip C. Schlechty boldly delineates why the focus on engaging students overrides the focus on test scores. Every teacher and administrator in my district will use this guide to transform our entire organization into one that is truly focused on student engagement. Years ago I read *Working on the Work* and it changed my teaching and leadership focus. This new work has extended my vision even more.

—*Kim Redmond, superintendent, Canton Local Schools, Canton, Ohio*

Dr. Schlechty has written another insightful book that reminds the reader that every decision made in schools should ultimately benefit students. Student engagement is explained in new and compelling ways and the book's clear message is useful for anyone who truly cares about students and the future of our country. You will find yourself referring to this book again and again as a guide to support you in your role as an educator or policymaker.

—*Allene Magill, executive director, Professional Association of Georgia Educators, Atlanta, Georgia*

This book presents a much-enriched framework for everything Dr. Schlechty advocates: well-articulated curriculum standards, schools as a platforms for learning, teachers as leaders and designers of engaging and meaningful work, and students becoming responsible for their learning.

—*Nyana Sims, K–12 literacy and induction facilitator, Goshen School District, Torrington, Wyoming*

Not since the release of *Working on the Work*, Schlechty's 2002 publication, have we had such an insightful guide to the transformation of our classrooms and student learning. *Engaging Students* embodies and reveals the learnings from countless hours of work with schools across the nation—pulling educators into new roles as designers and leaders. By understanding and implementing the principles so thoughtfully articulated here, schools can become centers of highly engaged learners—moving from compliant bureaucracies to learning organizations—and in that endeavor find again the joy of teaching and learning.

—*Johnny Veselka, executive director, Texas Association of School Administrators, Austin, Texas*

Engaging Students

THE NEXT LEVEL OF
WORKING ON THE WORK

Phillip C. Schlechty

JOSSEY-BASS
A Wiley Imprint
www.josseybass.com

Published by Jossey-Bass
A Wiley Imprint
One Montgomery Street, Suite 1200, San Francisco, CA 94104-4594—www.josseybass.com

Jossey-Bass books and products are available through most bookstores. To contact Jossey-Bass directly call our Customer Care Department within the U.S. at 800-956-7739, outside the U.S. at 317-572-3986, or fax 317-572-4002.

Jossey-Bass also publishes its books in a variety of electronic formats. Some content that appears in print may not be available in electronic books.

Library of Congress Cataloging-in-Publication Data

Schlechty, Phillip C., 1937-
    Engaging Students: The Next Level of Working on the Work / Phillip C. Schlechty.
      p.   cm
    Includes bibliographical references and index.
    ISBN 978-0-470-64008-1 (pbk.); 978-1-118-01550-6 (ebk.); 978-1-118-01551-3 (ebk.);
978-1-118-01552-0 (ebk)
        1. School improvement programs—United States.   2. Academic achievement—United States.
        3. Curriculum change—United States.   4. School environment—United States.   I. Title.
    LB2822.82.S344   2011
    371.2'07—dc22

                                     2010045736

Printed in the United States of America
FIRST EDITION
PB Printing   10 9 8 7 6 5

CONTENTS

ACKNOWLEDGMENTS

As with all my books I owe much to many people. First and foremost I owe much to the entire staff from Schlechty Center for Leadership in School Reform, a not-for-profit organization I founded in 1987. The mission of this center is to provide school leaders with support they need to carry out the difficult task of transforming schools. The books I write are written in support of this mission.

There are twenty-six staff members at the Center and all have contributed to this book. There are, however, five staff members who I feel obliged to provide whatever special recognition an acknowledgment in a book might provide. First, I want to thank Tena Lutz, who has assisted me in my work since 1984. Without Tena's assistance, I would not have finished most of the books I have written, including this one. Kim Vidrine, deserves a special thank-you for all of her tireless editorial work. She is both diligent and insightful.

Third, I would like to give a special thank you to Bob Nolte who has worked with me since 1990 and who always provides brilliant critiques of my writing. He always seems to know what I mean, even when I say it poorly. Fourth, I want to thank George Thompson, who is president of the Schlechty Center. One of the smartest things I ever did was recruit George to the Center and recommend that he be named president and chief operating officer. I can think of no person to whom I would rather entrust whatever professional legacy I might leave. His thoughtful critiques have been most useful to me.

I also want to acknowledge the very substantial contribution Lennie Hay, a staff member at the Schlechty Center, made to the development of this book. Among other things she wrote the first draft of all of the beginning sections of each chapter and identified the major concepts that appear in the box at the beginning of the chapter. She also made detailed comments on each chapter and helped me think through several issues with which I was having difficulties.

In addition to the staff members noted previously, I want to express my appreciation to a review panel that spent two days with me reviewing a nearly final version of this book. The members of this panel were Randy Bridges, superintendent, Alamance-Burlington (North Carolina) School District; Phillip Brown, principal, Whitfield County (Georgia) Public Schools; Angie Jacobson, teacher, Muscogee County (Georgia) schools; Gary Patterson, superintendent, Alamo Heights (Texas) ISD; Kim Redmond, superintendent, Canton (Ohio) Local Schools; David Reynolds, Professional Association of Georgia Educators; Nyana Sims, instructional facilitator, Goshen County (Wyoming) Schools; Kiara Wilson, teacher, Dayton (Ohio) public schools.

Finally, I want to thank the editorial staff at Jossey-Bass. I have written a number of books that that have been published by Jossey-Bass and have always been pleased with the help and support I received from the editorial staff. Those to whom I owe special thanks include Lesley Iura, associate publisher; Kate Gagne, acquisitions editor; Susan Geraghty, production editor; and Beverly Miller, copyeditor.

THE AUTHOR

Phillip Schlechty is the founder and chief executive officer of the Schlechty Center for Leadership in School Reform. He has been a teacher and public school administrator, as well as a university professor and associate dean. He established the Center for Leadership in School Reform in 1988; through this organization, he has developed a staff of experienced educators who are committed to transforming schools from bureaucracies into learning organizations. Schlechty and the center staff work with thousands of teachers, principals, central office staff, superintendents, and school boards, as well as with parents, civic leaders, business leaders, and others interested in the continuing health of public education in the United States. The center works with school districts across the United States.

Over the past forty years, Schlechty has written eight books and many journal articles dealing with issues related to the transformation of schools and school leadership. He has received awards from such diverse organizations as the American Federation of Teachers, the American Educational Research Association, and the National Staff Development Council. Most recently, his alma mater, The Ohio State University, honored him by inducting him into the School of Education and Human Ecology Faculty and Alumni Hall of Fame.

ABOUT THE SCHLECHTY CENTER

The Schlechty Center is a private, nonprofit organization committed to partnering with school leaders across the country to transform their classrooms, schools, and school districts from teaching platforms focused on compliance to learning platforms focused on engagement. The Schlechty Center provides educators with intellectual scaffoldings and frameworks to discipline action, training experiences, networking opportunities, disciplined discussions, dialogue, and advice on strategy and process. There are twenty-nine staff members who work every day to support educators in their efforts to transform education in America.

The activities of the Schlechty Center proceed from the assumption that if the schools are to be transformed they must be transformed by the men and women who are even now living out their lives in our schools. The goal of the Center is to provide ideas, support, and tools to those who are committed to this difficult journey. Many of these ideas can be found in the books written by Phillip Schlechty, but the Center's work is not limited to these ideas. Indeed, much of the work the Center does is based on the work of many other authors and researchers as well as the hard-won insights provided by the clients with whom the staff of the Center works.

PART ONE Engagement

Introduction

The metaphors we use to frame discussions reveal much about the mental models we hold regarding the subject being discussed. The metaphors commonly used to frame discussions about teaching almost always suggest the ideas that the teacher is a performer and that teacher performance is a key explanatory variable in the quest to understand what students learn in school. Indeed, the idea that the teacher is a performer and that the way the teacher goes about his or her work is a matter of central importance shapes much theory and practice in the study of teaching and the evaluation of teachers. Few educators have not heard of teacher performance appraisal systems, and few are unaware of the fact that a key element of such systems is the observed behavior of the teacher in the classroom.

Who the teacher is and what the teacher does is important to what students learn, and to suggest otherwise is foolish. I do, however, take serious exception to the notion that teacher performance is a cause and student learning is an effect. Teachers do perform, but it is not their performance that "causes" students to learn. Rather, it is the performance of the student that should be the assumed cause of learning. Instead of thinking of teachers as performers, I prefer to think of them as designers of experiences for students. I assume that the essential skills that teachers need are those associated with designing work for students that students find engaging. These skills include those that are essential to ensuring that the work is designed in a way that results in students' learning what it is intended that they learn.

In my view, it is much more important to assess the quality of the experiences teachers provide for students than it is to assess the quality of a teacher's performance. Indeed, I would argue that the assumption that the teacher's performance is the critical variable in student learning does great harm to both students and those who teach them. Teachers are leaders, and like all other leaders, they are best judged by what they get others to do than by what they do themselves.

Even if the assumption that test scores are fair representations of student learning is granted, which I do not grant, much more is involved in the scores students produce than those things the teacher does or fails to do. Teachers do not produce test scores; students produce test scores. Much that students learn and much that shows up on their completed tests they likely learned outside school, including at home where students and parents may actually talk, or fail to talk, about what the student is or is not learning. Should the teacher who has the good fortune of having parents who educate their own children be credited for being so lucky, and should those who have fewer of these parents be blamed? Nonsense!

There are really only two things that have the prospect of having a direct impact on student performance over which the teacher has any real control. First is the relationship that teachers have with their students and the way teachers, as leaders, treat their students. Second is the work teachers assign to students or encourage them to undertake. These two things, rather than the teacher's performance, should be central in our concern about the effect of teachers on student learning, for they determine what students do, and fail to do, as they carry out their lives in school. Effective teachers get students to do the right things, and they design things for them to do that are right for the students they teach.

Students do not learn from the performance of teachers; they learn from their own performance. The teacher's job is then to ensure that the students' performance optimizes the prospect that they will learn what they need to in order to participate effectively in American cultural, economic, and civic life.

THE PURPOSE OF THIS BOOK

This book was initially intended to be a modest revision of an earlier book I wrote: *Working on the Work: An Action Plan for Teachers, Principals, and Superintendents*. As I got into this task, it became clear to me that rather than a simple revision, what was required was an almost total rewrite, and thus a different book entirely.

Readers who are familiar with the earlier book will find much here with which they will be familiar. For example, in Chapters Seven to Nine, there are only slight revisions of three earlier chapters. Chapters Two through Five and

Chapter Ten, however, contain much new material as well as elaborations and expansions of ideas I presented in *Working on the Work*.

This does not mean that I have abandoned the ideas I set forth in the earlier book. I have not. Rather, my experiences over the past decade have helped me to clarify what I once said and caused me to rethink how to position what I suggested in the context of school reform initiatives today. Two matters have been especially significant in shaping my thinking about the issues I address in this book. First, as the original *Working on the Work* framework has become more widespread (the original version of the book has sold nearly 150,000 copies), it has become clear that what I wrote and what some people think I wrote are not always congruent. As the author, I accept responsibility for these misunderstandings. As I often said to some of my students, "You never know what you have said or written until someone tells you. All you know is what you intended to say or to write. The message received is more important than the message sent."

A second matter of considerable importance is the direction and development of the current government-sponsored efforts to improve education in the United Sates. When I wrote *Working on the Work*, the test-based accountability system that emerged out of the No Child Left Behind legislation was not yet fully developed. Standards-based accountability was being talked about, but standards had not yet morphed into scores on standardized tests. Clearly the standards that the early proponents of standards-based school reform envisioned (standards to which I had some attraction) are no longer the standards of concern. Rather than asking, "What should students know and be able to do?" we now ask, "What do students need to know and be able to do to reach a given cutoff point on an easily scored, relatively inexpensive standardized test?" The answer to this latter question becomes the standard of concern.

I have always believed that well-articulated curriculum standards are essential to the proper education of children. They both provide direction and impose needed discipline. Nevertheless, there is a difference between student performance standards—that is, standards regarding what students should be able to demonstrate that they know and can do—and curriculum standards.

Curriculum standards have to do with conceptions of the purposes of schooling and the ends of education. Student performance standards have to do with the immediate and the measurable. Curriculum standards and student performance standards are—or should be—related, but they are not synonymous.

Curriculum standards have to do with the desired and the desirable. Student performance standards have to do with the observable and the acceptable.

We do need clear and powerful curriculum standards. Indeed, I do not see how a school faculty can proceed without some agreement on what the curriculum standards are and without some means of enforcing these. However, I do not believe these standards necessarily flow from some state or federal bureaucrat's office and that the means of enforcement are the bureaucratic means available to governments. Standards, if they are to have meaning in a democracy, must be developed by local communities and enforced by them as well. Moreover, the means of enforcement must move beyond the formalized structures suggested by testing and into the arena of continuous examination of student learning outcomes and the work that students are provided in pursuit of these standards. If standards are to count, they must be embraced by people who count to students—and in the accounting of students, their peers, families, and teachers count for more than do governors, education bureaucrats, or even business leaders and foundations. To have standards-based schooling, therefore, one must seek as well a common core of standards in the community that the school or schools serve.

A GREAT MUTATION

In 1962 historian Carl Bridenbaugh, in a presidential address to the American Historical Association, coined the phrase *great mutation* to characterize a development he wanted to discuss. He said:

> The Great Mutation, or historical change, has taken place so rapidly, and life has sustained such sudden and radical alterations (in the long course of time) that we are now suffering something like historical amnesia. In the present century, first Western civilization and now the entire globe have witnessed the inexorable substitution of an artificial environment and a materialistic outlook on life for the old natural environment and spiritual world view that linked us so irrevocably to the Recent and Distant Pasts. So pervading and complete has been this change, and so complex has life become— I almost said overwhelming—that it now appears probable that mid-nineteenth-century America or Western Europe had more in common with fifth-century Greece (physically, economically,

socially, mentally, spiritually) than with their own projections into the middle of the twentieth century. Is it possible that so short a time can alter the condition of man?[1]

A member of the 1962 audience looking back over the past fifty years might well have said, "Carl, you ain't seen nothing yet." The changes that have occurred since 1962 make those that Bridenbaugh describes pale in significance.

Public schools as we now know them were established in the nineteenth century to fulfill for the masses an educational function that had heretofore been fulfilled by families, private tutors, and academies. The assumption underlying the early American school—usually referred to as the "common school"—was that the job of the teacher is to pass on the knowledge and lore of the "tribe." In this view, adults control children and what they will learn because adults control the information children will receive as a part of their education. The teacher is the master of this information and the primary point of access to the information. The student is a supplicant and a subordinate. Students are obliged to comply with their teachers' directives because parents, teachers, and schools represent the primary point of access to the collective wisdom of society. This view is deeply embedded in the tradition and lore that surround schools in the United States.

Such a view of the relationship between teacher and student has served tradition-based societies well. But it has become difficult to sustain this view in contemporary America where traditions are eroding and being replaced with new practices and new fads on a regular basis. And one of the most fundamental changes is that adults no longer control the access the young have to information. In the world of the Internet and mass media, students often learn things before their teachers or their parents are even aware of them. Sometimes what students learn is consistent with what adults want them to learn and sometimes it is not, but whatever the case, they do learn, and what they learn shapes the way they will live their lives.

Adults, whether parents or teachers, can no longer control the information students receive. (Even closed communities like the Amish are having difficulty in this regard.) Therefore, if schools and teachers are to continue to have a major impact on what students learn, teachers are going to need to learn to direct the learning of their students rather than attempt to control it. This means that

[1]C. Bridenbaugh, "The Great Mutation." *American Historical Review,* 1963, *68,* 315–331.

teachers need to rethink the way they have traditionally related to students. They can no longer depend on the superiority of their knowledge and wisdom (which still may be quite real) to help reinforce the authority that tradition has bestowed on them.

One way to help reconceive this relationship is to think of the student as a customer for work and the teacher as the designer of that work. Properly viewed, customers are at the center of any enterprise. Without customers, businesses do not exist. As Peter Drucker has observed, the primary goal of any business should be getting and keeping customers.[2]

Similarly, students are, or should be, at the center of schools and schooling. Engaging students in work that results in their need to learn material that is essential to their education as citizens in a democracy and to their right to claim to be well-educated human beings is the primary business of schools.

Students do not volunteer to go to school; they are compelled by their parents and the law to attend. Like it or not, however, students do control those things the teacher needs from them to ensure that the students will learn those things it is intended that they learn. Students control the effort they are willing to invest and the attention they are willing to pay. Sometimes it is possible to bribe students to "pay attention" and to invest effort, and sometimes they can be coerced to do so. However, if the attention they pay and the effort they invest is to result in quality learning, they must do more than comply. They must be committed to the work they undertake—so committed that they will stick with it even when they fail on initial tries and experience difficulties along the way. This means that they must be engaged in the work rather than simply compliant with its demands, and that means that the work must have inherent meaning for them. I wrote *Working on the Work* in an effort to help teachers become increasingly successful in designing engaging work. This book pursues the same end.

A WORD ABOUT CONTEXT

I wrote my first book on schools and schooling in 1975 and published it the next year. Even then I had concluded that instruction could not be improved until schools changed in fundamental ways. These changes must occur in the boardroom as well as the classroom, in the statehouse as well as the schoolhouse.

---

[2]See, for example, Peter Drucker, *The Essential Drucker: The Best of Sixty Years of Peter Drucker's Essential Writings on Management* (New York: HarperCollins, 2001).

In the years since *Working on the Work* was published in 2002, I have become much clearer about the nature of the changes needed.

Between 2005 and 2009 I wrote and rewrote a manuscript for a now-published book, *Leading for Learning*, in which I describe in considerable detail the kinds of changes I believe are necessary. *Leading for Learning*, however, is about redesigning schools and school districts, not about designing work for students. That book does not enter the classroom door other than by inference. Instead, it is an effort to set forth a set of propositions regarding the type of system that needs to be created if teachers are encouraged to work on the work.

Working on the Work was written before *Leading for Learning*, but *Leading for Learning* provides the context for that earlier book and probably should be read before turning to this one. Indeed, I believe that reading *Leading for Learning* can relieve some of the angst teachers sometimes feel when they first see clearly the kinds of changes they are going to confront if they take seriously the suggestions I make in this book.

Indeed, as I have watched bureaucratically mandated school reform initiatives play out, I have gained a new appreciation for the pressures these changes put on teachers and principals. All of this has served to reinforce something I have long understood to be true: the way schools are organized affects what teachers do in classrooms. So long as schools are organized as rational bureaucracies, teachers who are committed to creating engaging work for students will find it difficult to operate in the context of schools, and students will suffer because this is so.

As a result of these reenergized appreciations, I am now more firmly convinced than ever before that if teachers are to design more engaging work for students, those who control schools and the way schools operate must be prepared to design schools and school districts in ways that are supportive of this activity. Principals, superintendents, and school boards need to understand it. Most of all, policymakers bent on improving education through bureaucratization of processes and bureaucratized forms of assessment and accountability must understand it and stop doing some of the silly and misguided things they are now doing. They must, for example, abandon test-based, punishment-centered accountability and embrace the notion that sound pedagogy is based on beliefs and that standards are best thought of as sources of direction rather than weapons for maintaining control.

Rather than viewing schools as teaching platforms, schools must be viewed as learning platforms. Rather than seeing schools as knowledge distribution systems, schools must be seen as knowledge work systems. Rather than defining teachers as instructors, teachers must be defined as designers, leaders, and guides to instruction.

Just as Gutenberg's printing press made the role of scribes obsolete, e-learning and all that surrounds it are on the way to making the role of teacher as instructor obsolete. This most assuredly does not mean that teaching and teachers are obsolete or can be replaced by computers. Rather, it means that the role of the teacher as instructor is obsolete. But at the same time this information technology is creating an even greater need for teachers to embrace the role of leader, guide to instruction, and designer of work for students.

A personal story may make my meaning more clear.

My eight-year-old grandson is familiar with computers and how to access Google. One evening he and his mother were watching a television show featuring a trip to Belgium. After the show, Daniel went to his computer and looked up Belgium on the Web. Though it is not clear what he read, when his mother asked him what he learned, he responded, "Well, one of the things I learned was that the Belgians were very busy during World War II." When his mother asked him what made him think that, he said, "Well, the article said that during World War II, the Belgians were occupied by the Germans, so I just figured the Germans were keeping them busy."

Clearly Daniel had received instruction without the benefit of a teacher, but without a teacher (in this case, his mother) to guide him to understand what he had learned from his faceless instructor could well have been misleading indeed. Much of what I present in the pages that follow is aimed at helping teachers and those who work with them to think through the implications of this brave new world for teachers and teaching in the hope that that which is occurring even now will not result in an Orwellian nightmare and the loss of our precious democratic heritage.

THE ISSUE OF REDUNDANCY

For readers who are concerned about editorial matters, I want to point out at the start that this book contains considerable redundancy and that the redundancy is intentional. What I write in one chapter I repeat in a slightly different form in another. For example, in Chapter Two I present the Working on the Work framework and the language it suggests as a set of assumptions regarding the characteristics and attributes of work that teachers must take into account in the design of engaging work. In Chapter Five, I use the same framework as a structure for discussing ideas about prototypes and design specifications. Sometimes I discuss these ideas simply as design qualities, but at other times I move the discussion of these qualities well beyond that which will be known to those familiar with my earlier work on this subject.

There is a risk that in this way, I will add to confusion rather than bring greater clarity to my intentions. I believe, however, that the redundant use of some of these categories will better explain some of the subtle differences between designing work and planning lessons. Moreover, I am convinced that until teachers understand the difference between designing engaging work for students and planning interesting lessons, they are more likely to play at working on the work rather than work at it.

Finally, I want to acknowledge that I am aware that I make frequent and sometimes redundant commentary regarding the direction of government-sponsored efforts to reform schools. If I seem obsessed with this problem it is because so many of the teachers and principals with whom I work are so fastened on test scores that they find it difficult to think about working on the work and I want them to know that I understand the source of their distress. I am, however, convinced that unless teachers come to focus on engagement as much as so many now focus on test scores, there will be little improvement in our schools. Unfortunately, too many teachers believe that as long as they must contend with the ham-fisted use of standardized tests to ensure accountability, the expectation that they can also work on the work, though perhaps desirable, is unrealistic. I am not unaware of the problems my proposals create for teachers but I have confidence that much good can be done even now to change the course of school reform in this nation. One of the things that can be done is to help teachers articulate the problems they feel. I hope my commentary can be of use in this regard.

The Meaning
of Engagement

Key Ideas

- Assessing engagement
- Attention
- Commitment
- Compliance
- Engagement
- Highly engaged classroom
- Meaning
- Motivation

- Noncompliance
- Pathological classroom
- Persistence
- Profound learning
- Superficial learning
- Types of involvement
- Well-managed classroom

Jane, a fourth-grade teacher, sits at her desk at the end of the day and remembers a recent discussion about engagement and compliance in a faculty meeting. Her class this year presents no behavior problems and her students are eager to submit their work for Jane's evaluation. However, Jane worries that maybe most of her students are primarily interested in grades, winning a place on the school's honor roll, and having their work posted on the "Classroom Stars" bulletin board. Today, Jane described a new unit to her fourth graders. The unit was to be a departure from the science textbook. It would involve science investigation requiring teamwork, collection of water samples from a stream near the school, a partnership with a high school biology class and use of their lab, research about water quality, culminating in a classroom science magazine written by the students about their investigation and findings. Although Jane anticipated that her students would be excited about this learning experience, the first thing they wanted to know was how they would be graded. Their questions had to do with "points they would earn for each part of the unit," "number of pages each team would have to write," "number of research articles required," and the like. In frustration and disappointment, Jane spontaneously announced that the unit would be ungraded and the class would invite high school students, other teachers in the school, and, perhaps, some local environmental scientists to review their work and give them comments. The fourth graders were still not excited and asked if they couldn't just get back to their science textbook with its clear assignments and chapter tests. Jane leaves her classroom that afternoon perplexed.

*E*ngagement is central to this book, just as it should be central in the life of schools. It is important that readers be aware of the reasons I place engagement in such a central position in the constellation of my concerns about the future of public education in the United States. Because the term is now used in so many ways, it is also important for readers to have a clear understanding of what I mean when I use the word *engagement*. This chapter provides the information needed to ensure these understandings.

ENGAGEMENT DEFINED

Four components are always present when a student is engaged:

1. The engaged student is attentive, in the sense that he or she pays attention to and focuses on the tasks associated with the work being done.

2. The engaged student is committed. He or she voluntarily (that is, without the promise of extrinsic rewards or the threat of negative consequences) deploys scarce resources under his or her control (time, attention, and effort, for example) to support the activity called for by the task.

3. The engaged student is persistent. He or she sticks with the task even when it presents difficulties.

4. The engaged student finds meaning and value in the tasks that make up the work.

Sometimes on-task behavior is confused with engagement. On-task behavior indicates only that a student is attentive to a task. It says nothing of the student's willingness to persist with the task when he or she experiences difficulty. It also says nothing about the value the student attaches to the task or the meaning he or she associates with the activity related to it. A student might persist with a difficult task simply because he or she places value on some extrinsic rewards promised for successful completion of the task—for example, a good grade, admission to college, or eligibility to participate in extracurricular activities. Take the promise of these extrinsic rewards away, and the student is likely to abandon the task since completing it has no other meaning or value for him or her. For example, students who aspire to enter highly selective colleges are more likely to do whatever it takes to get a good grade than are students whose college aspirations are less lofty.

Even when a student is attentive and persistent, there is no assurance that the student is engaged. Engagement involves commitment as well as attention and persistence. Attention can be focused through fear and the threat of punishment, but those who are attentive because of fear and threat are not engaged. Neither are those who pay attention and persist because they place a high value on some reward that is extrinsic to the work. Commitment, attention, and persistence must be present to justify the claim that the student is engaged.

INVOLVEMENT AND ENGAGEMENT

Students who are engaged are involved, but not all students who are involved are engaged. The most critical difference between students who are engaged and those who are not is the way they relate to the situation or tasks at hand.

In the past, I posited five ways that a student might respond to a learning task:

- Authentic engagement
- Ritual engagement
- Passive compliance
- Retreatism
- Rebellion[1]

It has become clear to me, however, that these labels are sometimes misleading and confusing. Consequently I have relabeled some of the categories and have modified and elaborated some of the definitions. For example, I no longer speak of *authentic engagement*. Rather, I simply use *engagement*. Where once I spoke and wrote about *ritual engagement*, I now speak and write about *strategic compliance*. Where once I used *passive compliance* to indicate a response in which students do only the minimum required to avoid negative consequences, I now use *ritual compliance*. Table 2.1 summarizes these changes.

[1]This framework has been very much influenced by Robert K. Merton's discussion of modes of adaptation to norms in his *Social Theory and Social Structure* (Glencoe, Ill.: Glencoe Press, 1957).

Table 2.1
**Previous and New Terms for Student Responses
to a Learning Task**

Previous Term	New Term
Authentic engagement	Engagement
Ritual engagement	Strategic compliance
Passive compliance	Ritual compliance
Retreatism	Retreatism
Rebellion	Rebellion

Compliance suggests the willingness to do what is expected or required by a task. Involvement requires participation but it does not require compliance. There are, in fact, many students who are involved in school and attend classes yet are also alienated from school life and the way schools go about their business. Some are so alienated that they drop out as soon as they can do so legally. More often, however, students who do not find personal meaning in the work they are expected to do in school and do not find the extrinsic rewards either accessible or of significant value seek to reach a compromise with their teachers and their schools.[2]

Sometimes nonengaged students adopt a retreatist posture. As long as the teacher does not insist on some evidence of compliance, the student causes no problems. More often, however, because schools and teachers have, and are perceived to have, considerable influence over the way coveted extrinsic rewards are accessed and distributed, students make strategic decisions to comply with requirements even if they do not embrace them or find them inherently compelling.

Students who highly value the extrinsic rewards may expend a great deal of effort and be willing to persist with the task at least until they attain the reward.

[2]The basic structure underlying this framework is derived from Amitai Etzioni's distinctions among three types of involvement, which he labels *moral involvement, calculative involvement,* and *alienative involvement.* Although I have modified Etzioni's formulation a bit in order to make it fit the condition I am describing, I owe much to his original work. See his *A Comparative Analysis of Complex Organizations* (New York: Free Press, 1961).

Unlike students who find personal meaning in the work, however, those who are strategically compliant almost always have a conditional commitment to the work: they are willing to do the work only so long as the extrinsic reward is present. Remove the reward, and they withdraw the effort. (This is perhaps what is behind teachers' frequent complaint that students are often "working only for the grade.")

COMPLIANCE WITHOUT ENGAGEMENT

Recognizing that learning requires activity on the part of students, teachers typically seek to ensure that students are compliant even if they are not engaged. To some teachers, strategic compliance and ritual compliance are adequate. There are at least three reasons for this:

- Raising students' awareness regarding rewards and heightening their consciousness of negative consequences is a relatively straightforward task. Moreover, teachers generally have a well-developed set of understandings regarding the kinds of extrinsic rewards that students value and negative sanctions they are most likely to abhor. Teachers are much less certain regarding the causes and sources of engagement. Indeed, many see engagement as a responsibility of students, and they view students who are not engaged as remiss in their duties.

- The level and type of learning that standardized tests measure—which is increasingly the focus of teacher concerns—can usually be produced by strategic compliance and sometimes even ritual compliance.

- Many, if not most, teachers assume that student engagement has more to do with the sentiments and orientations of students than it does with anything over which teachers exercise control. In this view, good students are those who place high value on academic work done as academics would have them do this work. Students who are not as accomplished do not share these academic values, or so teachers sometimes argue.

It is certainly clear that extrinsic rewards and threats of negative sanctions can and do shape behavior. Most teachers also understand that the type of learning that occurs as a result of the systematic application of rewards and punishments may satisfy some short-term goals. However, it might not have the long-term effects that might be anticipated if students did what they were expected to do because they found the work engaging rather than doing the work as a result of calculative decisions regarding rewards and punishments. Indeed, teachers have been known to apply the label *grade grubber* to students who, they believe, work only for the grade.

The idea that engagement is more of a product of student attributes than of anything over which the teacher can exercise direct control also has some support in the experiences of teachers. Clearly some students find meaning, relevance, and significance in academic pursuits carried out in the manner that academics expect them to be carried out. These students have embraced and internalized the norms of the academy and are more likely than their peers to find schoolwork engaging. They have, in fact, become fully socialized to the idealized ways of the academy and find these ways morally compelling. They do what they must because they believe that they ought to do it and that it is just the right thing to do. They are, to use Amitai Etzioni's term, "morally involved."[3]

The type of involvement students have in school and the generalized meaning they attach to school experiences have an effect on the ease with which teachers are able to get students engaged. Morally involved students are easier to engage because they value the kind of work academics value. Traditional academic work, presented in traditional ways, can be engaging to such students. Indeed, it is the morally involved student to whom teachers often refer when they think of the "ideal student" or the student they would hold up as an exemplar. The problem, of course, is that many Americans do not find academic work, or the way academics go about their work, engaging. Thus we hear business leaders suggest that ideas are "only academic," and books and articles are written about anti-intellectualism in America. Populist commentators and politicians have a great time poking fun at the so-called academics and the intellectual elite.

FROM STRATEGIC COMPLIANCE TO REBELLION

Just as alienated students can sometimes be brought into compliance through coercion, students who are generally positively disposed toward school, especially those

[3]Ibid.

who are calculatively involved,[4] sometimes rebel. Indeed, one of the most difficult issues confronting teachers who are working in some high-performing schools (as measured by test scores) is that many of the students do not expect or even desire for their schoolwork to be engaging. What they want instead are certainty and predictability. They sometimes simply want assurance that whatever they do will pay off in grades and improved chances to enter the college of their choice.

There are, in fact, many examples of this phenomenon noted in the education literature. Edward Humes in his book *School of Dreams* notes one of my favorites. (Another is Elinor Burkett's *Another Planet*.) Humes's case is about a highly regarded physics teacher who decided to encourage his students to undertake a serious experiment that called on them to apply what they were learning to a concrete situation. The task required imagination and persistence and carried with it considerable likelihood of initial failure. The best students in the class—those who in the past did their assigned tasks with proficiency—rebelled. They insisted that the teacher return to textbook assignments and conventional tests because this was the world they knew and had mastery of and in which they were known "winners." They were interested in passing tests and said so. They did not have time to do physics. What they did have time to do was cram for a physics test on Monday so they could then cram for a math test on Thursday. When the teacher designed work that encouraged them to go beyond the predictable routines that they were comfortable with and had mastered, they refused to do the work and negotiated with the teacher to return to a more conventional format.

As this case illustrates, sometimes students are involved in the school and its activities not because they find life in school satisfying or full of meaning and significance. Rather, they have come to believe that their time in school will result in benefits they want to receive—for example, a well-paying job after completing college, happy parents, avoidance of the social stigma associated with being labeled a dropout, and so on. These calculative students are likely to engage in strategic compliance when the rewards are clear and resist (that is, rebel or retreat) when they do not see the connection between the activity and the reward. (The commonly asked question, "Will this be on the test?" is an example of strategic compliance.) If there is not a clear link between tasks and extrinsic rewards or

---

[4]*Alienative, calculative,* and *moral involvement,* as I am using the terms here, directly parallel Etzioni's typology in ibid.

if the student finds a more efficient means of achieving these values, compliance with the requirements of the task may deteriorate. In the extreme, this noncompliance can devolve into such things as institutionalized cheating.[5]

In contrast, a student who finds personal meaning in the work might engage in considerable self-initiated activity and even modify tasks if he or she thinks that those changes result in a high-quality work product. It is this fact, more than any other, that leads me to conclude that the goal of developing in most students the skills and habits of mind that result in creativity, the ability to solve complex problems and understand complex arguments, and the ability to approach tasks in a disciplined way cannot be achieved until and unless the work schools and teachers provide students is engaging to more students than is now the case.

Commitment and meaning transform involvement from an act of submission or ritual compliance to one of active involvement and investment of self. Without commitment, there is no engagement, and without meaning, commitment is not likely to occur. Moreover, without engagement, the likelihood that students will invest enough of themselves in the learning activity to truly construct, create, and discover (as contrasted with absorbing, assimilating, and imitating) is diminished greatly.

Learning academic things is important to most Americans, but many Americans do not find the way academics go about learning these things particularly inviting. Learning for learning's sake may be a part of the mantra of academics, but for most Americans, learning needs to have some motive beyond itself. For this reason, teachers must learn to design work that is engaging for students and requires students learn what their teachers intend.

RETREATISM AND REBELLION

Noncompliance is a fact of school life, just as certainly as is compliance. And like compliance, noncompliance takes on various forms. Whatever form it takes, however, noncompliance includes the fact that noncompliant students refuse to become involved in the tasks they are given. Some students manifest this lack of

---

[5]See, for example, "Students' Cheating Scheme Uncovered," *WRAL.com*, Feb. 26, 2008, which reports on a pattern of theft of tests that had been going on in a high-performing school, the Chapel Hill School in Chapel Hill, North Carolina, for many years. http://www.wral.com/news/local/story/2484284/.

compliance in passive ways: they retreat or withdraw from the work and its associated tasks and activities.

This retreatism often goes undetected, especially in classes where teacher performance rather than student work is assumed to be the causal mechanism for learning. (See Chapter Seven for a discussion of the assumption that teaching causes learning.) Students who retreat simply do nothing and bother no one. Sometimes those who retreat on a regular basis develop strategies to conceal their noncompliance. Bill Cosby once referred to students' "going to sleep with their eyes wide open," and I would add, "sometimes with a knowing smile on their faces." This behavior is not unknown in school, including graduate school. *Retreatism* seems an appropriate label for this type of noncompliance.

Rebellion, another form of noncompliance, is more active than retreatism. Students who rebel are not only refusing to comply; they are choosing to fasten their attention on other matters. And sometimes what they attend to is disruptive to the work of others. For example, a student who is so engaged in a social studies project from another class that he or she continues to concentrate on social studies in math class is de facto in rebellion, in spite of being highly engaged in work. (This sort of thing sometimes causes tension between teachers who are masters at creating engaging work and teachers who are less skilled in this regard.)

It is commonplace to suggest that students who consistently rebel or retreat are unmotivated or do not value learning. I do not believe this is so. Rather, I believe that all students value learning, and all students are motivated. The problem is that many students find little in what they are required to learn in school that has any meaning in the context of the motives they have. In order to address this problem, teachers need to have a deep understanding of student motives as well as an understanding of what they, and their students' parents, should want their students to learn. The art and science of teaching is found in the design of work for students that appeals to the motives they bring to that work and results in their learning what their teachers expect them to learn.

SUPERFICIAL AND PROFOUND LEARNING

There are at least two types of academic learning: superficial learning and profound learning. *Superficial learning* involves only short-term memory and provides little in the way of application in novel contexts. This learning is compartmentalized rather than embedded in worldviews and habitual ways of thinking and doing. It does not require much in the way of commitment, meaning, persistence, or voluntary effort. All that is required is student compliance and a means of inducing students to spend sufficient time on task to "master" the involved operations well enough to respond appropriately on tests.

Profound learning affects and shapes students' habits and worldviews. Knowledge and skills of this sort are transferable to contexts beyond those in which they were acquired or developed. Profound learning goes beyond the acquisition of facts and the memorization of propositions to include learning to evaluate facts and other supposed forms of knowledge and create novel arrangements of prior learning. Profound learning endures and leaves a residue of understanding that provides a cognitive framework to which other learning can be attached.

BLOOM'S TAXONOMY

More than fifty years ago, Benjamin Bloom and a group of psychologists and specialists in mental measurement developed a typology of learning objectives, commonly known among educators as Bloom's taxonomy, that they published in *Taxonomy of Educational Objectives*. The following list provides an updated and revised description of the essential categories Bloom and his colleagues used to describe educational goals and objectives in what they referred to as the cognitive domain:[6]

- *Creating*—putting together ideas or elements to develop an original idea or engage in creative thinking
- *Evaluating*—judging the value of ideas, materials, and methods through the development and application of standards and criteria
- *Analyzing*—breaking information down into its component elements
- *Applying*—using strategies, concepts, principles, and theories in new situations
- *Understanding*—inferring, exemplifying, classifying, and comparing
- *Remembering*—recalling and recognizing given information

[6]Bloom's initial frame subsequently was revised. The source of the listing presented here is L. W. Anderson and D. R. Krathwohl, *A Taxonomy for Learning, Teaching, and Assessing: A Revision of Bloom's Taxonomy of Educational Objectives* (White Plains, N.Y.: Longman, 2001). My definitions are generally those provided by these authors, although I have fleshed out some of the definitions more than one might find in the original. I have taken the liberty of paraphrasing some of the original statements to make them more consistent with the format I use here.

My own use of the framework differs in several ways from the way most other educators use it. First, I treat each of the six categories as descriptions of learning tasks rather than as statements of objectives or outcomes. Furthermore, I do not view any one of these categories as part of a learning continuum. In my view, the differences among these categories have more to do with the level and type of effort students might be expected to invest rather than the level of learning that might result. Committing things to memory is neither inferior nor a lower order of learning than is evaluation.

Second, I do not assume that accomplishment in any one of these areas is dependent on accomplishment in other areas. I do not assume, for example, that evaluation must be preceded by memorization. Certainly we want students to learn how to remember, but remembering what they learn is more important. Certainly we want them to learn how to evaluate, but examining what they know and what they think they know in the light of new learning and new evidence is more important. Moreover, when things they learn do not fit with what they know or think they know, we want them to wonder why and have the tools to help them find answers to this query.

Finally, I assume that when a student remembers an item in a profound way, the memory lasts and becomes embedded in a network of his or her other memories, each of which is connected and takes on meaning in the mental life of that learner. In contrast, a superficial memory does not last long. Moreover, it does not reshape thinking or cause cognitive dissonance. Superficial learning is called superficial because it skims across the surface. Profound learning goes deep into the cognitive frames students use to organize their world.

ENGAGEMENT AND EFFORT

When students are engaged, they are related to the tasks they are involved with in a different way than when they are strategically or ritually compliant. Among other things, the relationship between these students and their work is generally unconditional. They are committed to the task, and the commitment is not contingent on the presence of rewards that are extrinsic to the work or the threat of punishment or negative sanctions. There is, furthermore, a qualitative difference between the level and type of effort that engaged students are prepared to invest in their work and the level and type of effort of those who are only compliant. Students who are engaged are prepared to persist until they accomplish a satisfactory result. Students who are strategically or ritually compliant are willing to persist only if extrinsic rewards are clear and present or if the threat of negative sanctions is sufficiently onerous to worry them.

Engagement has become increasingly important because it is so integrally related to effort. Our democracy and our economy depend on citizens who have learned to think, reason, reflect, solve problems, and create. In the not-too-distant past, the type of education that might result in this type of learning was reserved for the elite. Today nearly every child needs an elite education. It is not enough to simply train the young so they can mark more right answers on a computer-scored test. Indeed, too much attention to test scores, especially on standardized tests, can distract attention from the need to engage students and can focus on strategies that produce compliance without engagement.

Memorizing material for the purposes of a test does require effort, but it is not the same kind or level of effort required when the intent is to produce memories that run deep and last—that is, long-term retention. Furthermore, willingness to persist with a learning task is more likely to be challenged by a task in which the outcome is uncertain and the processes poorly understood—as is the case with evaluating and creating—than in a task in which the outcome is more knowable and the means of doing the job more fully appreciated—as is the case with memorizing. It is, however, much easier to specify and describe outcomes and processes associated with memorization than it is to describe those associated with evaluation and creation. Moreover, typically evaluation and creation require concentrated attention over a relatively sustained period of time, whereas memorization of lists requires only sporadic investments of effort.

This is probably the reason that critical thinking, problem solving, synthesizing, and evaluating—all matters associated with what educators refer to as "higher-order cognitive skills"—seem to develop more often in the context of engagement than in a context in which students are doing the task assigned only because they are seeking rewards extrinsic to the work or fear negative consequences for failure to do the work. If this is so, and I believe that it is, then creating engaging schoolwork certainly has meaning for those who want to ensure that all students develop the skills they will need to survive and thrive in this century.

Partly because of these facts, engagement is becoming central to the idea of school and schooling. Twenty-first-century skills, whether these are rationalized in terms of economic need or civic requirements, require students to participate in much more complex learning tasks than is the case when learning outcomes are more in line with the requirements of less complex tasks. Engagement is more likely to produce the levels of persistence and commitment required to sustain the kind of effort needed to learn at higher levels.

ENGAGEMENT AND TRUST

If students are to be engaged, they must believe that their work will have meaning, even if the meaning is not immediately apparent to them. This is one of the reasons that building a trusting relationship between teacher and student is critical to designing engaging work. It is also one of the reasons that the skill of the teacher as leader is so critical. (Chapter Seven elaborates on this point.)

Though perhaps a bit counterintuitive, the fact is that students who are engaged in their work often volunteer to do tasks that are in themselves boring, humdrum, and routine. These students understand that doing such tasks is essential to participating in the larger piece of work in which they believe and to which they are committed. More than that, they trust that their teachers will not assign meaningless work.

When students do not trust their teacher, they are unlikely to work on tasks in which they have no personal interest or do not personally value unless some extrinsic reward or threat of punishment is present. The learning that will result may be adequate for purposes of a standardized test, but it will be unlikely to develop the understanding and skills required by the conditions of the twenty-first century. When they trust their teacher, they also trust that rote memory work is not always without meaning and the learning that results can be profound in the long run.

How do teachers communicate to students that they believe in them and trust them? There is no magic formula here. I have observed, however, that teachers who find the time to engage students in personal conversations and conduct interviews with students that reveal that the teacher wants to ensure that the work students are expected to do is engaging increases trust between students and the teacher. In one instance, a student told a member of the Schlechty Center staff that he never knew his teacher cared whether he found the work engaging. Now that his teacher is asking him about how he feels about the work he is assigned, he feels more like a partner with his teacher than a student, and he tries to "help the teacher think up ways to make the work more engaging." This is not a bad place to begin.

ENGAGEMENT AND ENTERTAINMENT

Schools are, or should be, serious places, but this does not mean that they are places lacking in joy, vitality, and even a bit of fun from time to time. To say that a school or teacher should strive to provide students with work they enjoy is not, however, the same as saying that the goal should be to entertain students or to make school "fun." Engagement does not mean entertainment—though properly framed engagement does result in enjoyment.

Entertainment is intended to distract attention. Engagement focuses attention. When fun is used to focus attention, it is not entertainment. Fun can be a mechanism for relieving tension or giving people time to pause in the midst of a tedious task or operation. Fun is not always frivolity, though it can be that. Fun provides for emotional release when tensions are high. (Humor is, by the way, one means of social control, to which any social psychologist will attest.)

By way of example, most readers will have heard speakers who use humor and stories to make a point and fasten attention. It is also likely that most of us have been in the presence of speakers who use humor and stories because they have no point to make or are not sure what they want the audience to pay attention to. The first speaker is trying to engage the audience; the second is simply entertaining the audience.

A teacher who feels that the only way to get students' attention is to entertain them clearly needs to begin to think more seriously about engagement. Students who are engaged do not need to be entertained. They and their teachers are getting too much joy out of what they are doing, and they are having fun while they do it.

ASSESSING ENGAGEMENT

It is not possible for a teacher to determine if a student is engaged by direct observation of that student's behavior at a given time, even though some aspects of engagement can be observed. For example, in conducting what is now being referred to as the classroom walkthrough, those conducting the walkthrough can observe on-task behaviors that provide a basis for reasonably inferring that students are paying attention. Persistence, however, is not so easily observed. Persistence has to do with sticking with the work or the task until it has been completed to a level that satisfies the ends that the task or the work is intended to satisfy. If the task is a relatively simple one, it might be possible to assess persistence through direct observation during a classroom walkthrough. If the ends of the task are more profound, persistence can be assessed only over time and will involve multiple observations as well as a good deal of interaction and conversation with the student doing the work. Similarly, commitment is not easily measured through direct observation. Determining why students invest energy, pay attention, and persist can be determined only through conversations with them. Sometimes students do the things they do because they find the activity has personal meaning and value to them, but more often they simply want to gain some reward extrinsic to the work or the work product or avoid some negative consequence if they do not comply. If a teacher wants to know whether students are engaged, he or she must consult the students themselves.

Finally, teachers and other observers can begin to appreciate the meaning that students attach to the work they are expected to do and the products, performances, and exhibitions they are expected to produce only through conversations and careful interviews. This requires that those who endeavor to assess student engagement first establish a trusting relationship with students. Otherwise students will not be willing to reveal what needs to be revealed to determine whether they are engaged.

The assessment of engagement should not be viewed as part of a bureaucratic evaluation system intended to render a judgment about the quality of the performance of the teacher. Rather, it should be viewed as a means by which school leaders and teachers who are committed to making engagement central in their schools make judgments about how they are doing in proceeding in the direction they have selected.

Given this view, the role of the teacher in assessing student engagement is critical. Indeed, the classroom teacher, more than any other person, is in a position to gain an accurate picture of the extent to which students are engaged in the work they are provided and encouraged to undertake. It is the teacher, after all, who is in a position to develop the kind of trusting relationships that will encourage students to provide honest feedback regarding their perceptions of the meaning and value of their work. He or she is in a position to assess the extent to which students persist with tasks when they have difficulty and discover what accounts for this persistence. Indeed, observing the lack of engagement (for example, off-task behavior) is easier than determining the presence of the other attributes that must be present if students are to be judged to be truly engaged as contrasted with being merely compliant.

The key to the assessment of engagement is the presence of teachers who truly want to know if their students are engaged and who are willing to accept the fact that even in the best of circumstances, not all students will be engaged all the time.[7] It is critical that teachers approach the assessment of engagement in their own classrooms, as well as in the classrooms of their colleagues, in disciplined and dependable ways. Assessments of engagement are team efforts. Each member of the team brings a unique perspective to the task, and these multiple perspectives are most likely to reveal the patterns of engagement in the most accurate and useful manner.

SOME ILLUSTRATIVE QUERIES

The best judges of student engagement are teachers. Outside observers can assist teachers and help them look more deeply into the data to which they have access, but only teachers are in a position to observe what is necessary for assessing student engagement. For example, only teachers can assess persistence and commitment because these responses require longer time frames for assessment. (They require a full-length movie rather than a snapshot.)

Teachers can become more disciplined in their efforts to assess engagement in their classrooms. One of the ways to develop this discipline is by crafting questions to routinely ask students even when the conversations seem to the student to be quite casual. Among the questions I have seen teachers use with great effect are these:

- Did you enjoy the class today? If so, what made it enjoyable? If not, what would have increased the level of enjoyment?

- Did you find any part of your work difficult? If so, what did you do? For example, did you just give up or settle for "this is the best I can do" and go on? How did you feel about what you did?

---

[7]Many teachers have developed questionnaires and other means of collecting data to assist them in making decisions regarding the presence or absence of engagement in their own classrooms, as well as tools they can use in cooperation with colleagues (including principals), in the attempt to bring the power of collective judgment to this effort. In the end, however, the utility of expending the effort to assess engagement will be determined only by the willingness of teachers to use the data they collect to improve the work they provide students so that more students are engaged more of the time and fewer students are never engaged at all.

- Why did you do the work you were assigned? Do you think you learned anything worthwhile from that work? If so, what and how could I know what you have learned?
- If you were to teach this class, what kind of activities would you build in, and why would you do that?

These questions are quite useful as tools to provoke students to participate in conversations that will reveal something of their motives as well as their reactions to the work they are assigned and encouraged to undertake.

DEVELOPING A CLASSROOM PROFILE

One of the first steps in moving toward improving the quality of the work provided to students is centering attention on the patterns of engagement in a classroom or set of classrooms. An individual teacher operating alone can do much to understand better what is going on in his or her classroom. For example, teachers can develop a profile of their own classrooms. Experience indicates, however, that until a teacher has had considerable practice in working with and thinking through this process, leadership and support by a principal and support from colleagues increase the likelihood that the teacher will stick with the process long enough to make it a routine part of his or her school life.

Generating the energy needed to sustain a group effort can take place in a variety of ways. One that I have observed to work well includes beginning with a workshop where the entire faculty is made aware of the basic ideas regarding student engagement. Following the initial workshop, principals are encouraged to work with volunteer teachers to develop engagement profiles of their own classrooms along the lines suggested by Figures 2.1 through 2.4. By making comparisons between two points in time (say, week 1 compared to week 2), teachers are able to see how patterns of engagement in their classrooms vary from day to day and task to task.

Engagement Profiles

The profiles that I set out here are based on a number of assumptions, the most important of which are as follows:

- Any given student will respond in different ways to different types of tasks, and sometimes the response will differ with regard to the same task. For

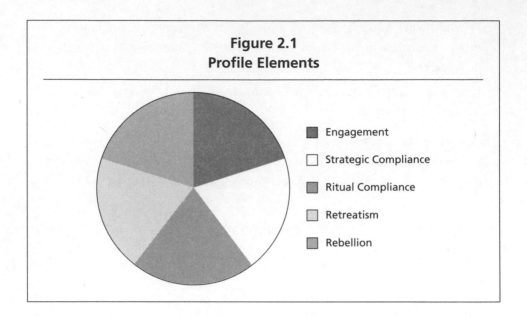

Figure 2.1
Profile Elements

- Engagement
- Strategic Compliance
- Ritual Compliance
- Retreatism
- Rebellion

example, a student who normally finds a task engaging may resort to retreatism on a given day or at a given moment because he or she is tired or distracted. Sometimes the same student may be ritually involved, and at other times the only thing that is compelling about the task for this student is what its accomplishment makes possible in another arena (perhaps eligibility to play football). The issue is not the presence or absence of these different responses but the pattern they create over time.

• Retreatism, ritual compliance, and strategic compliance are not in themselves indicators of pathology in the classroom. Furthermore, a student who is strategically complying, complying ritually, or acting in a retreatist mode is not necessarily misbehaving. In fact, it is not at all clear that anyone could tolerate—emotionally and physically—being engaged all the time. Retreatism may be a resting point for a student who has otherwise been engaged throughout the activity. Thus, the absence of engagement and the presence of strategic compliance, ritual compliance, and even some retreatism do not mean that classroom conditions are pathological.

• As schools are now organized, student success, especially success in doing well in an environment that places emphasis on high test scores, does not require engagement. In fact, many of the strategies that are being advanced to improve test scores are efforts to increase strategic compliance and ritual compliance and decrease retreatism and rebellion. Thus, classrooms can be well managed and even productive in terms of some measures of student learning without having achieved a high level of student engagement.

• Each of the types of response represents a different type or category of response rather than a different point on a continuum. A student who is strategically complying responds in a different way from a student who is engaged. Those who are strategically complying are not necessarily less diligent in carrying out required tasks than are those who are engaged. Rather, they are responding as they do for a different reason or set of reasons, and their willingness to respond as they do is likely to be more conditional. Similarly, ritual compliance is a distinct type of response, not a diminished form of strategic compliance. Unlike engagement or strategic compliance, however, ritual compliance is likely to be motivated more by avoidance of punishment or unpleasant consequences than by any type of positive goal or outcome.

• It is assumed that different types of responses to schoolwork produce different types of commitment and therefore different types of effort and learning results. I proceed from the hunch that students who are strategically compliant learn what they need to in order to do well on tests and satisfy the demands of adult authority; however, they probably retain less of what they have learned than would be the case if they were engaged. Indeed, students who are strategically compliant are likely to be so concerned with what is going to be on the test that they will be reluctant to undertake any task that does not have some clear payoff in terms of extrinsic values associated with such performance measures. The reason engagement is so important is that it contributes to long-term learning, persistence in learning complex material, and commitment to apply new learning to products.

• The type of conformance produced by ritual compliance is always more fragile and conditional than is the conformance produced by strategic considerations, just as strategic compliance produces a form of conformance with expectations that is less robust than is the conformance produced by engagement.

In the effort to describe the pattern of a given classroom, it would be a mistake to substitute precision of measurement to power of insight. The intent should be to gain a disciplined understanding of one's own classroom with regard to engagement and to submit superficial impressions to as rigorous a test

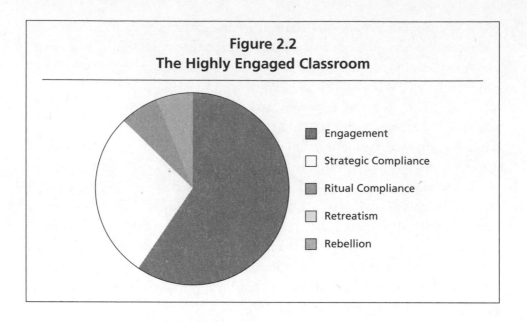

Figure 2.2
The Highly Engaged Classroom

- Engagement
- Strategic Compliance
- Ritual Compliance
- Retreatism
- Rebellion

as available data will allow. In the main, the intent is to raise consciousness about the need for more engagement and to provide a basis for making crude estimates regarding the level of success that has resulted from the present effort.

The Highly Engaged Classroom   In the highly engaged classroom (Figure 2.2), most students are engaged most of the time. There is, however, considerable strategic compliance, some ritual compliance, and maybe even a limited amount of retreatism. Rebellion may also occur in the highly engaged classroom, but it will be idiosyncratic and will not be sustained long enough to be patterned. In summary, most students in the highly engaged classroom are engaged most of the time, and all students are engaged some of the time. It is also a classroom that has little or no rebellion, limited retreatism, and limited ritual compliance.

The Well-Managed Classroom   Strategic compliance and ritual compliance are the dominant modes of response in well-managed classrooms (Figure 2.3). As in highly engaged classrooms, there is little or no rebellion. Because such a classroom is orderly and most students seem to do the work assigned—some with enthusiasm—it is easy for the teacher and outside observers to confuse the

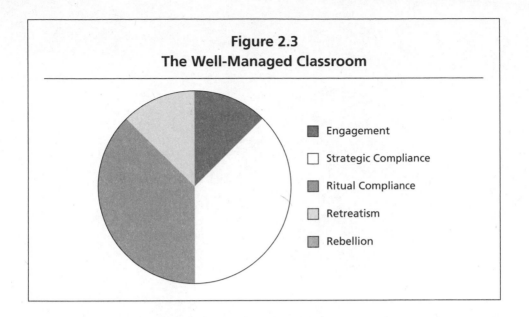

Figure 2.3
The Well-Managed Classroom

- Engagement
- Strategic Compliance
- Ritual Compliance
- Retreatism
- Rebellion

well-managed classroom with the highly engaged classroom. The well-managed classroom appears well managed not because students are engaged but because they are willing to be compliant.

In the Schlechty Center's work with teachers from across the country, teachers report that the well-managed classroom is the most common profile of classrooms. As long as the teacher and the principal fail to ask the right questions of students, the absence of engagement will probably go unnoticed, though the effects on learning may be quite real.

The Pathological Classroom The pathological classroom (Figure 2.4) looks very much like the well-managed classroom except for the presence of patterned rebellion. The rebellion is not limited to isolated cases. Many students actively reject the task assigned or substitute some other activity to replace what has been officially assigned or expected. (Cheating is a form of rebellion.) Furthermore, it seems likely that in the effort to reduce rebellion, teachers in the pathological classroom often settle for retreatism or ritual compliance and "work on the students" to gain such a response. Indeed, although I have no empirical evidence, I would bet that teachers in pathological classrooms tend to lower performance expectations to the point that ritual compliance gets higher rewards (better grades) than would be produced

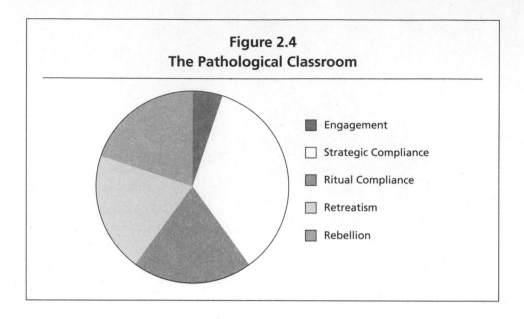

Figure 2.4
The Pathological Classroom

- Engagement
- Strategic Compliance
- Ritual Compliance
- Retreatism
- Rebellion

in a highly engaged classroom. This could be one source of the grade infla-tion that is of such concern to some critics of public schools. Nevertheless, there is likely to be some degree of engagement in the pathological classroom. For example, the subject being taught may be of such interest to a particular student that he or she finds meaning in even poorly designed tasks. There is likely to be considerable strategic compliance as well; some students need a good grade to get into the college they want, or they so fear displeasing their parents that they do whatever they need to do to get the teacher's approval. The incidence of ritual compliance will also be high, as will the incidence of retreatism. Indeed, it is the increase in retreatism and the presence of patterns of rebellion that distinguish the pathological classroom from the well-managed classroom.

Indicators of Responses to Work

In the effort to help teachers and other educators assess the presence or absence of engagement and to develop a classroom or school profile to guide action, I have developed a list of possible indicators of engagement, as well as the other four reactions that I have suggested might be used to characterize student responses to the work they are expected to do:

Engagement Indicators

- The student is attentive to the task because he or she finds personal meaning and value in the task; the student sees the task as responding to motives and values he or she brings to the work.

- The student persists with the task even when he or she experiences difficulty and does not compromise personal standards for completion of the task even though he or she might be able to negotiate a lower standard if he or she wanted to.

- The student volunteers resources under his or her control—time, effort, and attention—which is to say that the student is committed to the work and places moral value on its completion.

Strategic Compliance Indicators

- The student is attentive to the task because he or she perceives that the receipt of some desired extrinsic reward is conditionally available to those who pay attention to the task and do what is required of them.

- The student persists with the task only up to the point of ensuring that the desired reward is offered, and the student is willing to accept the reward and abandon the task even though he or she may not be personally satisfied that the work done is of the quality that he or she could produce.

- The student allocates only as much time, energy, and resources as are required to get the reward offered or desired.

Ritual Compliance Indicators

- The student pays minimal attention to the work, is easily distracted, and is constantly seeking alternative activity to pursue. For example, it appears that texting has now become a favorite pastime for those who are ritually compliant.

- The student is easily discouraged from completing the task and regularly tries to avoid the task or get the requirements of the work waived or compromised.

- The student does only those things that must be done and does little or nothing outside the context of direct supervision by the teacher or other adults.

Retreatism Indicators

- The student does not attend to the work, but does not engage in activity that distracts others. Indeed, the student often employs strategies to conceal his or her lack of involvement—for example, sleeping with eyes wide open and smiling from time to time.

- Because the student does not do the work, persistence is totally lacking.

- The student does nothing and, when forced through direct supervision to do the task, either engages in ritual behavior or rebellion.

Rebellion Indicators

- The student overtly refuses to comply with the requirements of the task. This refusal may involve cheating, refusing to do the work, or even doing other work in place of that which is expected.

- Because the student does not do the work, persistence is totally lacking.

- Alienation rather than commitment is evident. Unlike the retreaters, students who rebel are likely to be active in their rejection of the task, up to and including efforts to sabotage the work, cheat, and build negative coalitions of other students around the work and the rejection of the values the work suggests.

WHERE IS THE RESEARCH?

At this point, some readers may be asking, "But where is the research?" As will be seen in a later discussion of the work of Daniel Pink (see Chapter Three), the author of the book *Drive*, a number of studies support the assertion that when students are involved in tasks that have personal meaning to them, they are more likely to internalize, retain, and use in other contexts what they have learned by doing the tasks. Engagement is, of course, not the only way to create conditions in which students learn. Learning does result from activity induced by extrinsic rewards and threats of negative consequences. Nevertheless, the evidence suggests that the learning that results from extrinsic inducements is more likely to be superficial than profound and is as likely to do harm as to be beneficial. Moreover, this kind of learning is likely to require less complex mental operations—that is, learning that results from some of the less complex tasks that Bloom described in his taxonomy of educational objectives.

The idea that student engagement is central to profound learning is one of the most basic tenets of constructivist notions about instruction and is at the heart of what some refer to as a discovery approach or an inquiry approach to teaching. It is central to some highly sophisticated curriculum projects that have been developed since at least the 1960s. Engagement not only embraces the idea that learning is an active process; it holds as well that if learning is to be retained and made transferable, the tasks that result in the learning must have meaning to the learner. Moreover, it holds, as do most constructivists, that the type of learning that is required to encourage students to create and evaluate is qualitatively different from that which results in enhancing short-term recall.

In today's test-driven environment, however, the question, "Where is the research?" is often no more than a code for, "What effect does engagement have on test scores?" Over the past decade other members of the Schlechty Center staff and I, and teachers and administrators who work with us, have produced considerable anecdotal evidence suggesting that in schools where principals and faculty concentrate on creating engaging lessons, the rate of improvement in test scores is no less than it is in other comparable schools, so there is clearly no loss incurred when engagement is attended to.

The "we're no worse than anybody else" argument is not, however, persuasive. Unfortunately, common systems of testing today, especially standardized tests, do not even attempt to tap or describe intellectual work habits and problem-solving skills. Nor do they assess the skills needed to engage in collaborative work, which many see as a key concern for the twenty-first century. If schools and teachers spend most of their time implementing instructional strategies intended only to produce compliance (as they are now too often encouraged to do) without attention to engagement, the likelihood that students today will develop twenty-first-century skills and habits of mind is almost nil.

Even more to the point, teachers and other school leaders seem to think that the strategies they use to improve test scores do not result in much long-term retention. If this is not so, why then do they spend so much time and energy in conducting reviews and test preparation exercises? What all this attention to testing and test-taking skills probably indicates is the uncertainty teachers have about the long-lasting effects of what they are doing in the classroom and the certainty they have regarding the fact that they are more likely to be judged in terms of short-term effects than long-term consequences.

Based on many interviews with students from schools it is clear that attention to the quality of the work students are provided can have a profound impact on the way students view their work and sometimes their relationships with their teachers. When teachers clearly focus their attention of designing engaging work for students, many students report that they are very much aware of the efforts their teachers make to engage them and that they respond favorably to these efforts. One student said, "Until my teacher started asking me questions about my engagement, I didn't even know I was supposed to be engaged. Now I try to help my teacher create more engaging work for all of us." More than that, students routinely report that the efforts their teachers make to design engaging work have resulted in their increased willingness to enthusiastically embrace the tasks with which they are presented and have encouraged them to persist with even difficult and otherwise onerous tasks.

The real problem is that when the goal is to improve test scores and the test is focused primarily on lower-order learning with no real concern about long-term retention and transfer, teachers are not encouraged to seek to engage students in their work. Compliance produced by extrinsic rewards or by threats of negative consequences is a most efficient tool, and it fits neatly into the bureaucratic ethos of those who create the policies and the tests that now give direction to America's schools, as I noted in one of my previous books, *Leading for Learning*.

Consequently, good teaching is coming to be defined as teaching that efficiently, effectively, and reliably increases scores on tests that call for only a superficial grasp of relatively low-level knowledge. These tests may call on a student to write brief descriptive paragraphs about the poems others have written (which can then be reliably scored using an established rubric), but these tests cannot assess the ability of the student to write a poem or the willingness of the student to persist with this work when his first, second, and even third try do not satisfy either him or his audience. If we want students to create and evaluate as well as list, define, recognize, repeat, summarize, and compare, we must create ways of assessing creativity and evaluative skills.

As things now stand, many teachers with whom I work comment that although they would like to give their students more engaging work and would enjoy teaching more if they could spend time designing such work, they have standardized tests to worry about and therefore cannot afford to spend time on designing engaging work for students, even if it does produce more profound learning. The message I receive from teachers too often goes like this: "We [teachers] have more important things to do than worry about student engagement—things that will affect our survival and our school's reputation. Those things can be most efficiently produced through attention to doing what we have always done, which is to focus on getting students to do what we tell them to do even if that has no meaning to them."

Students too sometimes embrace the notion that schools are places where superficial learning is more valued than is profound learning. For some students (and their parents), learning how to take the test is becoming a more highly valued skill than is learning those things that students might need to know if they were to have a profound understanding of the items that appear on the test. Indeed, students often assert that they have no time to work on intellectually engaging tasks because to do so would distract them from covering the material they must to satisfy the conditions of the test.[8]

If we were truly concerned about students' developing twenty-first-century skills, policymakers would find ways of signaling to schools and teachers that they really care about such skills. This implies that the assessment system now in use will need to be totally revised and some means will need to be found to make the measurement of higher-order learning and profound learning at least as prominent as is the situation today with lower-order learning of a superficial sort. This cannot be done through mass testing, of course, so this means that much of what is now called *assessment* in education will once again need to be entrusted to local schools and local teachers.[9]

---

[8]A report in the *New York Times* suggests that the dominance of testing is invading even the lives of three- and four-year-old children whose parents seem willing to submit the children to "test prep" programs so that their offspring can matriculate into elite public kindergarten programs. See Sharon Otterman, "Tips for the Admissions Test . . . to Kindergarten," *New York Times*, Nov. 20, 2009.

[9]I am not unaware of the problems associated with what I am hinting at here, and I address these problems in my recent book *Leading for Learning*. The essential argument boils down to one proposition: it is not the business of the state to assess students but rather to assess the assessment that school districts use. When school districts have in place clear assessment processes that local teachers own, good things happen. When this is not the case, the good that happens is likely to be random, and the harm is likely to be systematic. State assessments of students do not send the signals to teachers and schools that must be sent if we want high-quality educational opportunities for all children. Strong assessments by teachers, peers, and parents are the only means of establishing a culture of excellence in which engagement is expected. The kind of learning likely to be produced by bribery and coercion is not enough.

PART TWO The Framework

Motives and Motivation

Key Ideas

- Algorithmic task
- Assumptions of framework
- Autonomy
- Design
- Extrinsic motivation
- Heuristic task

- Intellectual work
- Intrinsic motivation
- Mastery
- Planning
- Purpose

David causes his seventh-grade team teachers much concern. To all indications, he is bright and verbal, a reader, and a leader with his peers. However, he fails to turn in his daily homework, does poorly on weekly tests, seems preoccupied, and appears to daydream throughout most class presentations; he's barely making average grades. The only time this year he has shown any enthusiasm about class work is when students were asked to make a speech about some area in which they were expert. David used his laptop and made a compelling speech about his expertise with computer games.

As the final bell rings every day David races out the school doors. He retrieves his cell phone hidden in his backpack and accesses his Facebook page to look for new postings. He checks for messages from his gamer friends and plans to get on his computer as soon as possible. His books, papers, and school newsletter are a jumble in his backpack, and he quickly forgets about studying for the social studies test tomorrow. Achieving more points on the game he finds engaging is how he plans to spend his evening.

Why do students do what their teachers ask them to do? There are at least three answers to this question. First, students may comply with the directives of their teachers out of respect for traditional authority or out of fear of punishment if they fail to comply. Adults sometimes complain that students no longer respect adult authority, but much that happens in school occurs because most students accept the right of adults to direct them. Respect for adult authority is deeply embedded in our culture.

Second, students may perceive that the receipt of some extrinsic reward is contingent on their compliance. Because adults control most of the resources available to serve as rewards for students (including adult approval of performance), the ability of adults to shape the behavior of students through the judicious use of carrots and sticks is clear and is commonly used. For example, teachers often view grades as motivators, sometimes schools provide trips to amusement parks as incentives for performance, and some have even gone so far as to pay students for doing their schoolwork.

Third, students may simply find the work enjoyable and personally satisfying. They complete their assignments to satisfy their motives that are based in values they have learned to hold. When students behave in this way, they are said to be *intrinsically* motivated, meaning that they find their rewards to be inherent in the work rather than provided by some source external to the work. Intrinsic motives are essential to engagement and profound learning.

INTRINSIC AND EXTRINSIC MOTIVATION

In his book *Drive,* Daniel Pink has presented one of the most useful discussions of the distinction between extrinsic and intrinsic motivation and the reasons that intrinsic motivation should be a central concern in schools as well as in businesses. Beginning with a distinction between extrinsic and intrinsic motivation similar to the one I just presented, Pink presents a research-based argument that challenges many traditional assumptions regarding motivation. He is highly critical of the use of extrinsic rewards as a means of inducing desired behavior and improving performance and outcomes, especially when those outcomes require creativity, problem solving, and other complex mental operations. The bottom line of his argument is that although reliance on extrinsic rewards and the threat of punishment sometimes produces increases in performance, it more often does not achieve this end and quite often suppresses performance, especially when the performance requires creativity, problem solving, and novel framing of issues. Intrinsic rewards, however, are clearly related to increases in productivity, especially when these increases require creativity and problem solving.

Pink identifies three types of drives. Type 1 is based in biological needs, such as the needs for food and sex. Type 2 drives are those that can be satisfied with rewards that are contingent on behaving in a proper way or avoiding behaving in an improper way. These rewards are controlled by others or by the environment and can be accessed only by compliance with the requirements of these others or by adjustments to the external environment.

Type 3 drives emerge as a result of human need for such things as autonomy, mastery, and purpose. Implicitly at least, Pink argues that autonomy, mastery, and purpose are key elements in the design of engaging work. He goes on to provide numerous useful examples of work that is responsive to these needs and is therefore intrinsically motivating.

He does not, however, indicate how the design of intrinsically motivating work differs from the design of work that requires extrinsic motivation, other than to say that the work is designed in a way that responds to the need for autonomy, mastery, and purpose. Moreover, it becomes clear that Pink may not be talking about the work at all; rather, he may be addressing the context in which the work is done and the results of doing work that is designed in a way that produces intrinsic motivation.

For example, Pink says autonomy is the opposite of control. I find this a strange definition of autonomy. Autonomy has to do with who and what is controlled rather than the presence or absence of control. In a work environment, autonomy has to do with the context in which work is done and the relationship of the worker to the work. Autonomy implies control by self rather than control by others. It means that the worker has control over his or her work and over the way the work will be done. The need that is to be satisfied is the need for control.

Those who act autonomously are not out of control. Rather, they find their sources of control in principles they have chosen and a discipline they have internalized. Indeed, autonomy, if it is to lead to satisfying results for the worker and others, requires disciplined pursuit of a continuously more demanding standard.

Mastery has to do with standards of quality, "the desire to get better and better at something that matters."[1] Work that inspires mastery is designed in a way that focuses attention on clear performance standards that are inherently compelling to the worker. The worker must learn to value the standard or standards by which mastery is to be judged before mastery can be used as a motivator.

[1]Daniel Pink, *Drive* (New York: Riverhead, 2009), p. 111.

Although Pink clearly demonstrates that mastery is not encouraged by extrinsic rewards, we are left with the question, "What does work that encourages mastery look like, and how does it differ from work that must depend on extrinsic rewards?" Moreover, mastery requires a great deal of effort, so another question is, "What would lead students to do something that takes so much effort?" Perhaps it is challenge that provides the incentive. If so, what are the characteristics of challenging work?

Finally, although I agree with Pink that purpose is an important aspect of work, the question remains, "What leads students to impute purpose to some forms of activity and not to others? What does activity that inspires a sense of purpose in workers look like, and how does this activity differ from activity that does not inspire a sense of purpose?" It is, after all, a sense of purpose that gives work its meaning.

The question of purpose has to do with an even more important question: "Whose purpose?" Engaging work—work that is intrinsically motivating—serves the purposes, ends, and values that a student brings to the task. Sometimes school activity serves purposes the teacher has in mind but does not respond to the intrinsic motives and values of the student. In such cases, gaining student compliance becomes the end in view, and sometimes the consequences are awful to behold. The following story, told recently by a member of the Schlechty Center staff who is also a mother, is but one illustration:

> My mother was in town visiting us not long ago. One night while I was downstairs in the kitchen, I overheard a conversation taking place upstairs. My mom tries to engage my daughters in all sorts of wonderful conversations when she's with them. That evening's topic was, "What's your greatest fear?" My oldest daughter, who is a wonderful student, barely hesitated when she was posed the question. "Missing the CATS test" was her answer. She was referring to the state's standardized testing system here in Kentucky. My mom asked for clarification: "What is the CATS test? What do you mean 'missing it'? Getting a bad score?" Helen responded that she was referring to being absent on one of the testing days; she followed up with her reason: "If you miss a day of the test, *you'll never be able to get a good job in your life*." [Emphasis added by the author.] Helen went on to say that her two other greatest fears are dying and the devil.

Note that missing the standardized test beat out those two. Regardless of your thoughts on the afterlife, you have to admit that that's really something. It's also remarkable that Helen couldn't think of a few other things to be more afraid of—for example, she suffers from epilepsy, has occasional bouts of crushing insomnia as a result of her seizure medications, has been hospitalized for pneumonia and a broken leg, and is frequently subjected to lab work and blood testing ordered by her neurologist. On top of that, she worries more than most other fourth graders, I'd suspect, about issues of both global and local significance—everything from the Somali pirates to how to get more people in the world to stop smoking. And yet missing a day of the state's standardized test is the scariest thing in the world to her. Wow.

This story illustrates how powerful extrinsic rewards can sometimes have effects on students that are potentially quite harmful to students, even high-performing students. In Helen's story, the ham-fisted use of extrinsic motivators frightened this child more than the devil and dying. Surely a point or two on a standardized test is not worth this much pain. Ironically, frightened children probably do worse on the test than if they had been left alone.

Students who find schoolwork intrinsically motivating almost certainly learn more and do better than those who find no source of intrinsic motivation in their schoolwork. In the typical school system today, however, the definition of a good student is too often limited to those who are intrinsically motivated by schoolwork designed to require students to do knowledge work in the manner that academics do it.

Academic work done the way academics do it is only one form of knowledge work, and it is not the only kind of intellectual work that results in the mastery of academic subjects. Not all intellectuals are academics, and not all academics are intellectuals. Knowing how to create art and music, solve problems, envision new solutions to problems, and reframe problems is not limited to academics or the academic way of doing work. Indeed, leaders outside the academy have been known to speak disparagingly of styles of knowledge work that they label as "too academic." The styles of the academy are not the styles of the rest of the world, nor should they be. Furthermore, the style of the academy is not the only style that can result in the mastery of knowledge valued in the academy as well as in the rest of the world.

If we want more students to be more engaged and more intrinsically motivated to learn academic subjects and see how mastery of those subjects can help them do things they care about, we need to design schoolwork differently. We need to honor many forms of intellectual work that currently are not honored in the narrow definition of what matters in school. Certainly we have a better chance of redesigning the work we provide to students than we do of redesigning children, their parents, or the environment from which the children come.

DESIGN VERSUS PLANNING

Over the past ten years, the ideas of design, design thinking, and strategic thinking have swept the business world. And as frequently happens when business leaders become fascinated with an idea, these ideas find expression in education as well.

There are many important distinctions between planning and design. The following are those that I have found most important:

- Design begins with customers and the needs of customers. Planning begins with goals, objectives, programs of action, and activities.
- Design assumes divergence, disruption, and chaos. Planning assumes convergence, linearity, and order.
- Design is expressive and embraces values and emotions. Planning is instrumental and embraces deductive logic and rational analysis.
- Design is controlled by principles, product specifications, client values, and client response. Planning is controlled by rules, procedures, goals, and predetermined results.
- Design emphasizes divergent thinking. Planning emphasizes convergent thinking.
- Design seeks alternatives and invites invention. Planning seeks to limit alternatives and encourages conformance to rules, time lines, and codified procedures.
- Designers synthesize and unify. Planners analyze and segment.

Perhaps the most important distinction between design and planning is that design is what social scientists refer to as a heuristic task, whereas planning is an algorithmic task. Pink puts it this way: "An algorithmic task is one in which you follow a set of established instructions down a single pathway to one conclusion. . . . A heuristic task is the opposite. Precisely because no algorithm exists for it, you have to experiment with possibilities and devise novel solutions."[2]

Two of the most fundamental problems with the usual efforts to improve schools is that teaching is viewed as an algorithmic task and the conceptions of what motivates teachers and students are based on nineteenth- and early-twentieth-century thinking regarding human motivation. Teaching, in fact, is a heuristic task. Teachers must be encouraged to embrace uncertainty and thrive on chaos rather than impose a foolish certainty on what is an uncertain enterprise. Best practice cannot be described once and for all time; it must be discovered and created over and over again.[3] Teachers must learn to increase the rewards they build into the work rather than assuming that rewards extrinsic to the work are the keys to improved performance. Similarly, those who would motivate teachers to do these difficult tasks must seek ways of making the task of teaching more intrinsically motivating than is often now the case and cease relying on extrinsic rewards such as merit pay as a means of bringing about improvement in the quality of teacher performance.

This is not to say that extrinsic rewards and planning are irrelevant or unnecessary. As Pink has observed, it is first necessary to ensure that baseline rewards are adequate and fair and that they are perceived to be so. If the classroom environment is not inviting and exciting, no amount of rewards, either intrinsic or extrinsic, will suffice to offset the negative and suppressive effects of a hostile or sterile learning environment. If the school environment is not supportive of the design of engaging work, only a few heroic teachers will make the effort, and even these teachers are likely to burn out quickly.

Make no mistake: design is not undisciplined activity. It requires hard work and persistence, along with tolerance of ambiguity and experimentation. Design is activity disciplined by principles and results rather than externally imposed rules, procedures, and programs. It is a highly personal and idiosyncratic undertaking, disciplined by a common purpose and a common language that those involved in the design have come to share. Common purpose and common

[2]Ibid., p. 29.

[3]Among the clearest statements I have found regarding these matters is an interview with David Kelley: Claus von Zastrow, "New Designs for Learning: A Conversation with IDEO Founder David Kelley," *Public School Insights*, Jan. 20, 2010.

language bind together teachers who are committed to pursuing the creation of engaging work for students. And it is this common purpose and common language that provide the building blocks for an engagement-focused school.

Unfortunately, the language most teachers have been taught to use to talk about their task is that of bureaucrats and planners rather than the language of design. Teachers are taught to speak of goals, objectives, and time lines rather than of motives, needs, and values. They speak of measurement more than prototypes and data more than ideas. The language they use is often instrumental and cold as opposed to expressive and inviting. Students are products rather than neophytes to be inducted into the ways of knowledge work, and teachers are professional employees rather than leaders of children and of parents and communities.

Teachers are taught to make rational selections among alternative activities rather than to create new alternatives. They are encouraged to use predetermined formats and structures rather than to think metaphorically, creatively, and reflectively about the work they are trying to get students to do. Indeed, most of those who instruct teachers in the construction of lesson plans suggest that the first step in planning is to identify the learning objective. The second is to select appropriate activities, materials, and instructional processes. Only then should they consider students' motives and needs. Yet we insist that we are, or should be, student focused!

It is not to discount the importance of being clear about the intentions of instruction that I suggest that if teachers were to function as designers, they would need to be much clearer than today's system of schooling encourages them to be about who their students are, what motives they bring to the classroom, and what values they hold. Motives provide the context for instruction. If the activities teachers design do not respond to students' motives, students will not learn what their teacher intends, regardless of the clarity of the learning objective and the logic of the lesson plan.

To fully use the technologies that are now available to support students as learners and knowledge workers, teachers must see themselves as designers of work for students rather than planners of instruction. They will need to accept that much of what they now do when they instruct students can be better done by electronic means. Even the teacher's own lectures might be more useful as sources of instruction if they were recorded, edited, and made transportable. There are thousands of lectures available electronically that touch on many of the subjects taught in schools. Moreover, these lectures are often presented by leading college professors who are well in front of anything that will appear in textbooks within the current decade. In the future, teachers will need to be knowledgeable about these sources of instruction and be prepared to guide students to them just as they now guide them to resources in the library.

Most of all, teachers will need to adopt or adapt a way of thinking about what they do that gives emphasis to motivation and design—just as the language they now use centers attention on instruction and planning.

A LANGUAGE FOR THE DESIGN OF ENGAGING WORK

For over twenty years, I have been interested in developing a conceptual framework that could help teachers answer the question, "What characteristics of schoolwork do students find engaging?" As a result of pursuing this interest, I have developed a framework that has come to be known as the Working on the Work framework. It sets out ten qualities of work that seem especially important to the creation of engaging work for students:

Ten Design Qualities for Creating Engaging Work

1. Product focus

2. Content and substance

3. Organization of knowledge

4. Clear and compelling standards

5. Protection from adverse consequences

6. Affiliation

7. Affirmation

8. Novelty and variety

9. Choice

10. Authenticity

In my earlier work I referred to these as design qualities. These qualities, and the assumptions on which they are based, are outlined in the following section.

Product Focus

If schoolwork is to have coherence and meaning for students, the activities students undertake must focus on a product, performance, or exhibition that —

transforms meaningless activity into engaging work. Creating engaging work for students is the first step in·Working on the Work. Indeed, this creative act makes it possible to design work for students rather than to simply plan activities for them to do.

Content and Substance

Often some students have no interest in the subject they are being asked to study or master. In this case, the teacher is left with four alternatives:

- Provide extrinsic rewards sufficient to induce strategic compliance or ritual compliance.
- Work to make the subject more interesting.
- Abandon the effort to teach this material to students on the grounds that student interest in the subject is essential.
- Make the work more interesting even if the subjects that must be studied to do the work are not in themselves of interest to the student.

The first of these options, providing extrinsic rewards, can work under limited circumstances, but as Pink shows, the results are highly variable and often counterproductive. The second option is available only to teachers who are unusually well versed in the subject being taught or those who are themselves engaging personalities, and even then, these teachers run the risk of substituting entertainment for engagement. The third option fails to recognize that there may be some things students need to know in which they have no inherent interest, and some of these things may never be of interest (or utility) to them.

The final option is therefore the one I support for I believe it is more likely that all teachers can learn to design work that will engage all students than it is to ensure that every teacher is personally engaging to every student. For the teacher, the key is to design the work in a way that students want to do it, even if this means they must learn some material they might not elect to learn if what they need to learn were not relevant to the work they were trying to do.

Working on the work does not assume that students know better than their teachers what they need to know. Rather, it assumes that students do know, sometimes better than their teachers, what they are willing to do. Designing work that students want to do and that results in their learning what they need to learn is at the heart of great teaching.

Organization of Knowledge

The knowledge and skills that students need to do the work successfully should, when possible, be organized in a way that is responsive to the motives students bring to that work. The learning styles of students—rather than the instructional style of any given teacher—should determine how instruction should be delivered. When this is not possible or when the intent is to help students to learn new styles of learning, then it is important for teachers to seek other motivators to build into the work. Without motivators, students will not be likely to persist in learning new ways of learning. The world of disciplined knowledge will be forever forbidden to students if they do not learn new ways of learning and knowing.

My view is that the most basic civil right in a democratic society is the right to be enlightened about the many ways of knowing. The learning styles with which students are comfortable may not be the ones they need in all circumstances. It is a mistake to let students' preferred learning styles dictate the way knowledge will be organized, though these styles should be honored when it is possible to do so without violating the intentions of the work.

Clear and Compelling Standards

Standards apply to products, exhibitions, and performances. Regardless of the content or focus of the standard, the standards that have to be met must be clear to the student. Moreover, if these standards are to serve as sources of motivation for students, students must perceive them as meaningful, relevant, challenging, and attainable. If students feel that the standards have no meaning or are irrelevant to them, are not challenging, or seem to be unattainable, students' needs for purpose and mastery will not be served. In this case, the only alternative is to induce performance through the use of extrinsic forms of motivation.

Protection from Adverse Consequences: Separating Punishment from Failure

Challenging work always carries the risk of failure. Students do not mind failing; what they do not like is being punished for failure when they try. When students are punished for failure, they learn to avoid failure by becoming only ritually engaged in work that challenges them. If they instead are to pursue mastery, they must be protected from the adverse consequences of failures, especially failures on early tries. (Too often, speed of performance is more highly valued in school than is the quality of the work product. Too often, single trial learning is more highly valued than is mastery after persistent tries.)

Affiliation

Students are often more motivated to do work when they do so in the presence of and in cooperation with others. Moreover, when what they learn is perceived to contribute to others or to some performance, exhibition, or product they are creating with others—for example, a group project—their engagement is likely to be increased. Students, like adults, are social beings, and they value group effort.

Unfortunately, because most schoolwork is designed as activities to be completed by compliant individuals rather than as tasks to be mastered in order to do some engaging work, students who are quick and precocious often learn to dislike group work in school. Because these students can complete their assigned tasks without cooperation with others, those who are less quick and less precocious become a handicap to them rather than a resource.

Group work is not, however, work that is done by five or so individuals working independently together. It is interdependent and requires collaboration and cooperation. The young woman who pitches using a fast-pitch softball depends on the catcher and could not do what she needs to do if the catcher fails to do what she must do. If affiliation is to serve as a source of motivation for students, then group tasks must be designed so that collaboration with others is essential to the successful completion of the task. Any task that can be done by one person operating alone probably should be.

Although group work is often more productive than individual work, working in groups is hard work and requires considerable skill. Moreover, it requires considerable individual effort, and sometimes this effort is expended out of the sight of the group to which the work contributes. For example, I am sitting alone writing these pages, but eventually my colleagues will use what I write to develop training materials for use in Schlechty Center training. I will get considerable satisfaction out of the fact that my colleagues, for whom I have high regard, will take what I do as a contribution to their own work and the work of the Schlechty Center as a whole. Thus, what sometimes appears to be lonely work really involves the presence of many others, even if these others are present only symbolically.

Affirmation

Affirmation is more than teacher praise. It encompasses concrete feedback that informs the student that he or she is making progress. Indeed, one of the major design features of many computer games is the affirmation built into them. Players know where they stand and that their efforts count, and this knowledge keeps them trying even when they initially experience failure. One of the most powerful ways of increasing the ability of schoolwork to engage students is to ensure that affirmation is built into the work.

Affirmation is more than praise and positive feedback. It includes providing students with clear indications that what they are about is important and that they are important to what they are about. The students' contributions, as well as the relative merit of their performance, must be affirmed. Making students aware that others who are important to them value their contribution is perhaps the most important way that affirmation can be exploited as a motivational source.

Novelty and Variety

Novelty and variety are important elements in the design of engaging work. Surprise and fun are a vital component of the design process, and they are important elements in engaging work as well. But too much of even a good thing is not always good. Routine often causes performance to deteriorate, and novelty and variety can serve as a motive force or a distraction. When used as motive forces, novelty and variety are relevant aspects of work design. When used to distract, they are the tools of entertainers rather than designers.

Choice

Choice is a critical element in design and in any other effort to ensure that novelty will be built into the tasks students undertake. Being given the right to choose how they will go about their work can do much to motivate students to work on products, performances, or exhibitions about which they have had little choice, just as providing choice regarding products, performances, and exhibitions can do much to motivate students who have no choice in how they will do the work.

I am not arguing that students should always be provided choices in what they do or how they do it. Rather, I am saying that when choice is denied, some substitute motivators need to be created. The drive for autonomy is powerful, and the motives that must be satisfied to overwhelm this drive must be powerful as well.

Authenticity

Understanding the world as students see it is important to the design of engaging work. Not only can these perceptions be used to make the work more engaging, but these perceptions also shape the way students will respond to the work. For example, teacher praise, which is sometimes an affirmation, can also serve as a source of punishment for a student who fears losing status with his or her peers for being too compliant with the commands of adult authority. Indeed, until the culture of the school has developed to the point that performance on school tasks is valued in the peer culture of students, there is little likelihood that many of the symbolic rewards the school has to offer will work well—even as extrinsic rewards.

As most teachers know, students' peer culture shapes and gives meaning to events at least as much as do the other realities of school life. Thus, in designing work, teachers must take these cultural phenomena into account and use them where they can. They certainly should not design the work in ways that amount to a direct assault on these peer values and the norms these values support.

A CONCLUDING STATEMENT

Variance in learning outcomes that are attributable to the abilities students bring with them to school are beyond the control of teachers and schools. As one wag said, parents are sending schools the best children they have. However, I proceed from the assumption that effort is at least as important as native ability as an explanation for variance in learning outcomes. By attending to the qualities or attributes of the work they provide to students, teachers can enhance the prospect that more students will be engaged and for more of the time. Increasing the level and quality of the effort students invest in their work will increase learning outcomes.

If education is a lifelong process and the purpose of school is to provide students with the tools and habits they will need to stay the course, then designing engaging work is central to all teachers' missions. I hope that the framework presented in this chapter provides a basis for productive discussions and productive work among teachers who are committed to becoming increasingly proficient in designing engaging work. The remainder of this book is intended to help in this regard.

The Engagement-Focused School

Christine, a twenty-year veteran elementary teacher, sits in her classroom at the end of the day and looks at Classroom Standard 1: Engagement and the related questions that her principal has provided each teacher. She opens her journal, a familiar black-and-white composition notebook, and jots down her reflections about her classroom. As part of her personal commitment to grow in understanding about an engagement-focused school and classroom, Christine has decided to spend time during the first semester reflecting on each of the twelve classroom standards applied to her own classroom. She believes her principal who says that each teacher's reflection and internal dialogue are encouraged but not required.

Given Christine's experiences over the years, she is drawn to the notion of student engagement and wants to think through what it might mean for her classroom. She believes that much of what passes for learning these days is based on coercion and that students find little pleasure or satisfaction in their work. Learning more about engagement gives Christine hope for her students and herself.

Beliefs shape visions, and visions drive missions. Visions are not accomplished; they are realized. Missions are sets of goals that must be accomplished for visions to be realized, as I noted in one of my previous books, *Inventing Better Schools: An Action Plan for Educational Reform*. Beliefs are statements on which one is willing to act.

BELIEFS UNDERLYING WORKING ON THE WORK

These are statements of the beliefs and assumptions on which the Working on the Work framework is based:

1. Students are customers, volunteers, and knowledge workers. What they have to volunteer is their attention and commitment.

2. The primary role of teachers is that of designing engaging work for students and guiding them to the sources of instruction they need to do this work successfully.

3. Differences in the level and type of engagement directly affect the effort that students expend on school-related tasks.

4. Effort affects learning outcomes at least as much as it does intellectual ability.

5. The level and type of engagement vary depending on the qualities teachers build into the work they provide students.

6. Therefore, teachers can directly affect student learning through the invention of work that is most engaging to students.

One of the first steps in transforming a school into a learning organization is engaging the faculty in a serious consideration of these beliefs. Although the local context determines the way these beliefs will be manifested, some general conditions are certainly in evidence. Regardless of how a faculty reacts to these specific beliefs, whatever beliefs they embrace will need to address the issues identified in these six statements. For example, the beliefs need to address the role of students and teachers, views regarding the causes of learning, and views about the way teachers can shape what their students learn.

If faculty cannot reach consensus on these beliefs, they should articulate the reasons this is so and suggest alternatives. In this regard, I have found the concept of students as volunteers the most problematic of these statements, especially for some high school teachers. A second notion that is likely to produce some heated discussion is the idea that teachers can directly affect the effort their students expend by designing engaging work. Some teachers insist on holding on to the idea that motivation is a matter of student character. If a student is not motivated to do the work, the problem is with the student, not with the tasks he or she is expected to do. These teachers would say they should work on the students to ensure students behave as if they are motivated to do the work even when they find little in the work that inspires them.

I believe that students should be thought of as volunteers; I also think that one of the most important beliefs is that the characteristics of the work students are assigned directly affect their effort. Moreover, I suspect that the reason these beliefs are sometimes difficult for some teachers to embrace is that these statements represent a dramatic departure from the mental models that currently shape much thought about teaching and learning. Therefore, serious conversation around these beliefs should occur even if the discussions are sometimes difficult, perhaps even acrimonious.

THE ENGAGEMENT-FOCUSED SCHOOL: A VISION

Once a faculty has settled on a statement of beliefs, especially a statement of what they believe about the role of teachers and students, the next step is to create a picture, image, or story line that indicates what the school would look like if these beliefs were acted on.

The following are among the things that a school faculty embarking on the Working on the Work journey might explore and discuss. Taken as a whole, these statements define a vision of a school that is truly focused on engagement, and discussion of them will certainly identify many of the issues that must be raised if schools are to be transformed.

The reader will note that these statements are very similar to the framework presented in Chapter Three. There are, however, some differences. For example, I have added Patterns of Engagement and Student Achievement to the list of descriptors because I do not see how it is possible to envision a school without attending to these matters. Designing work, which is the subject of Chapter Three, is intended to increase engagement and achievement, but engagement and achievement are ends not means. The design qualities listed in Chapter Three are a means to an end. I have also broadened the idea of protection from adverse consequences to concern with a safe environment more generally. I have done this because I have learned that without trust teachers cannot work on the work and students are less apt to respond to the work that teachers design.

Standard 1: Patterns of Engagement. Nearly all classes are highly engaged. When they are not, teachers make every possible effort to redesign the pattern of activity in the classroom to engage more students.

Standard 2: Student Achievement. Parents, teachers, the principal, and the board of education, as well as others who have a stake in the performance of the schools, are satisfied with the level and type of learning that are occurring.

Standard 3: Content and Substance. Teachers and administrators have a clear, consistent, and shared understanding of what students are expected to know and be able to do at various grade levels. This understanding is consistent with such official statements of expectations as state and local standards. Teachers and administrators also have a reasonable assessment of student interest in the topics that these expectations and standards suggest.

Standard 4: Organization of Knowledge. Teachers and support personnel such as media specialists generally endeavor to ensure that the materials used to present information, propositions, ideas, and concepts to students are organized in ways that are most likely to appeal to the largest possible number of students and to ensure that students have the skills needed to use these materials.

Standard 5: Product Focus. The tasks students are assigned and the activities they are encouraged to undertake are clearly linked in the minds of the teacher and the students to performances, products, and exhibitions about which the students care and on which students place value.

Standard 6: Clear and Compelling Standards. When products, performances, or exhibitions are part of the instructional design, students understand the standards by which they will be evaluated. The students are committed to these standards and see the prospect of meeting them if they work diligently at the tasks assigned and the tasks they are encouraged to undertake.

Standard 7: A Safe Environment. Students and parents feel that the school as well as each classroom is a physically and psychologically safe place. Success is expected and failure is understood as a necessary part of learning; there is mutual respect between and among faculty and students; and the fear of harm or harassment from fellow students and demeaning comments from teachers is negligible.

Standard 8: Affirmation. People who are significant in the life of the student, including parents, siblings, peers, public audiences, and younger students, are positioned to observe, participate in, and benefit from student performances, as well as the products of those performances. They affirm the significance and importance of the activity to be undertaken.

Standard 9: Affiliation. Students are provided opportunities to work with others (peers, parents, other adults, teachers, students from other schools or classrooms) on products, group performances, and exhibitions that they and others judge to be of significance.

Standard 10: Novelty and Variety. The range of tasks, products, and exhibitions is wide and varied, and the technologies that students are encouraged to employ are varied as well, moving from the simplest and well understood (for example, a pen and a piece of paper) to the most complex (for example, sophisticated computer applications).

Standard 11: Choice. What students are to learn is usually not subject to negotiation. Nevertheless, they have considerable choice and numerous options in what they will do and how they will go about doing those things in order to learn.

Standard 12: Authenticity. The tasks students are assigned and the work they are encouraged to undertake have meaning and significance in their lives today and are related to consequences to which students attach importance.

Disciplined Conversations

When educators speak of discipline, it is usually in reference to students—for example, that one of them is a "discipline problem." There is, however, another meaning for the word. As used here, the word *discipline* has to do with the idea of regimen or a regularized manner of approaching a problem or task. Disciplines have a point of view. The botanist is concerned with the world of plants whereas the zoologist is concerned with the world of animals. Neither is right or wrong. They are simply different and require different tools, categories, and language to help scholars to think and talk about the matters that concern them.

The function of disciplines is to ensure control and coherence. To say that one is disciplined in the sense the word is used here is to say that one proceeds from a coherent point of view that suggests where one might look for answers when things get "out of control" or do not happen the way it is assumed they should. Thus, the school standards I have outlined describe a new vision for school and are a key tool for any faculty wanting to move in the direction these standards indicate.

The Working on the Work framework is what Rosabeth Moss Kanter, a highly regarded expert on organizational change, refers to as a "process discipline." She writes:

Process disciplines establish control that does not constrain. Total quality management (TQM) programs, for example, provide a common set of analytic and problem-solving techniques to be used in every part of the organization, regardless of the sub-disciplines involved in particular functions like engineering or marketing. The "inspiration" part of quality programs (leaders encouraging quality values) is often less important than the "perspiration" component (people using analytic tools to manage difficult trade-offs on their own). Process disciplines such as planning routines or problem-solving techniques guide action without constraining the form that action takes. And it is easier for people to work together when they share such disciplines.[1]

The beliefs and standards I have outlined are tools to help discipline the conversations that must go forward to transform a school into an engagement-centered organization. They invite faculties to create a school that has a purpose quite different from those that can be pursued in a bureaucratic, control-oriented system. Used consistently and collectively, the twelve school standards can provide school faculties with such a discipline.

Thus, I argue that to make conversations about engagement and patterns of classroom operation most productive, principals and teachers probably need to pursue answers in a systematic way. This does not mean that they need to go down the list and answer each question in order, although as a guide to private reflection, this might not be a bad idea. What they do need to do is understand that all of these questions deserve attention. The answers to some questions will be so obvious that little time will need to be spent on them. For others, it may be necessary to spend considerable time finding data on which to base whatever answers there are to be found.

Here, a word of caution is in order: sometimes the obvious answer is not the best answer. For example, teachers sometimes overestimate the amount of engagement in their classroom and sometimes even see retreatism as a form of ritual compliance. Indeed, I have found that as teachers become more familiar with the Working on the Work framework and more skilled in the use of the tools associated with it, they also become more self-critical. For example, teachers

[1]Rosabeth Moss Kanter, *Rosabeth Moss Kanter on the Frontiers of Management* (Boston: Harvard Business School Press, 1997), pp. 159–160.

who are beginning this process commonly believe—or say they believe—that most students are engaged most of the time in their classes. But as they gain experience with the Working on the Work framework and the concept of engagement, their estimates of the level of engagement diminish considerably. (Although there is not yet sufficient research to indicate what that level should be, I have taken to saying, "If all of your students are truly engaged half of the time and at least half of the students are engaged at any point in time, you are probably doing better than most of us do most of the time.")

If teachers really want to understand the patterns of engagement in their classrooms, they have to learn to ask students about these matters. Such matters cannot be understood through casual observation. Systematic interviews and probing discussions are required. They must ask students why they did the work they did. They need to ask probing questions that provide students the opportunity to express the meaning they attach to the activities they undertake and reveal the effect, both positive and negative that they have toward the form of work they are provided.

The answers that one student will provide to a question will often be very different from the answers another person or group will provide. Some activities (for example, monthly dialogue sessions and peer observations) are intended to help reveal these differences in perceptions. In pursuing these activities, as well as any other effort to apply the framework suggested here, it is important to keep the following in mind:

- This framework is not a lesson plan format. Seldom will all of the qualities and attributes listed be present in any given lesson on any given day. Furthermore, some of these attributes may not be present at all. In fact, the presence of the attribute is not what is at stake here. What is at stake is student engagement. The absence of an attribute becomes an issue only when the level of student engagement differs from that which is required.

- Opinions are data, but opinions supported by additional data are better than opinions that lack such support. Thus, the principal who has a wider view of the school may see things lacking in the operation of the school that teachers, isolated in their own classroom, might not perceive. When this happens, some strategy needs to be developed to help teachers gain a wider view of the school. For example, the principal might encourage teachers to shadow students or spend some time observing the work of the principal.

- Many of the data needed to answer the questions cannot be gained by direct observation in classrooms. To answer these questions fully, principals need to engage teachers and students in conversation, and teachers need to engage each other and students in conversation. Sometimes these conversations will be informal chats; sometimes they will result from formal interviews, focus group interviews, or discussions in faculty meetings.

- The data teachers gather about their own classrooms or the data a principal gathers schoolwide should never be used in an evaluation process. These data are meant to inform teachers in order to learn about engagement and then design work for students. These data are meant to inform principals about the current state of the school in order to lead others in realizing an engagement-focused school. The utility of such data as a tool for improvement will likely be compromised if it is used as the basis for some bureaucratically prescribed evaluation process.

- Once a significant cohort of faculty members and the principal fully embrace this framework, it becomes a lens through which almost all that teachers and principals see in the school and in classrooms (their own and the classrooms of others) will be viewed. They will find themselves asking if these attributes are present, and if they are not, whether their presence would enhance the prospect that more students will be engaged and more will be taught the "right stuff." When this happens, Working on the Work has become a habit in the school.

FRAMING THE DIALOGUE

Two types of dialogues must go forward if the values, beliefs, myths, and lore (culture) are to be transformed into a culture that supports the notion that Working on the Work is "the way we do business here." First, internal dialogue must occur as each person talks to himself or herself about his or her own situation, own role, and personal views regarding these matters; this is dialogue as personal reflection.

The second form of dialogue involves conversations between and among individuals and groups. Sometimes these conversations are between peers and sometimes between a teacher and a principal. Sometimes they involve only two people and sometimes the entire faculty. Generally such conversations are much more productive when they are disciplined by a common set of questions that provide focus and direction to what is being discussed. Indeed, without such questions, what promises to be a dialogue can become an argument where rhetoric more than reality and opinion more than fact become the currency of the realm.

The questions in the following sections have proved useful in helping faculties begin the conversations required if Working on the Work is to move from interesting words and slogans to a program of action. These questions are framed in a way that focuses on school-level concerns.

Individual teachers will need to adapt them to fit their classrooms. (The Appendix provides a detailed illustration of such an adaptation.)

Standard 1: Patterns of Engagement

- Are most students, most of the time, engaged in the tasks they are assigned?

- Do teachers intentionally plan the work they provide to students in ways that reflect attention to building in those qualities that show the most promise of increasing engagement?

- When the pattern of student engagement differs from that which teachers want or expect, do teachers analyze the work provided to discover what might account for the difficulty? Or do they instead seek first to explain away the lack of engagement as due to factors beyond their control?

- Do teachers commonly work together to analyze the characteristics of the work they are providing students? Do they provide each other with assistance and advice regarding ways of making the work more engaging to students?

- Is there evidence that over time the level of engagement has increased and rebellion, retreatism, and ritual compliance have decreased?

Standard 2: Student Achievement

- Are there solid data on which to base judgments regarding student achievement?

- Are the data available sufficient to persuade those who need to be persuaded (parents, teachers, community leaders, state officials) that they have an accurate picture of the level of student achievement in the school?

- Are parents satisfied that their children are progressing as they believe they should and learning what they need to?

- Are those who receive students from the school (middle schools in the case of elementary schools, high schools in the case of middle schools, institutions of higher education and employers in the case of high schools) satisfied that students from the school have learned what they needed to in order to succeed in their future environment?

- Do students who have attended the school believe that they learned what they needed to while in attendance? Do they have an overall favorable judgment of the quality of their experience in the school?

Standard 3: Content and Substance

- Can teachers and principals articulate what students under their tutelage are expected to know and be able to do?

- Are teachers and principals in agreement regarding what students are to be expected to know and be able to do?

- Do the ideas, propositions, and facts that are presented or made available to students reflect the best understandings of experts in the fields of concern? Are they consistent with the views and lines of argument presented by scholars in the relevant disciplines?

- Have the faculty and the principal conducted a careful review of standardized tests (local and state sponsored) to determine the content that officially proscribes and prescribes what students are to learn?

- When the faculty is in disagreement with the official standards used to assess student performance, do they make their views known to those who have promulgated them, as well as to parents and others who are in a position to influence such decisions? If educators are to be effective in this regard, they must become much more adept at the art of persuasion in the public forum than is now the case. Whining and hand wringing will not reverse a trend that has political force behind it. Clear arguments supported by facts are required. Developing alliances with school board leaders, union leaders, and local business leaders is essential. (For elaboration of this point, see my book *Leading for Learning: How to Transform Schools into Learning Organizations.*)

- Do teachers provide students with a wide range of activities that call on them to work with content and processes that have been identified as worth knowing and worth mastering?

- Do teachers take into account how their students are likely to respond to specific content so they can either reframe the content or ensure that other dimensions in the work they design will make the content engaging?

Standard 4: Organization of Knowledge

- Do most teachers clearly take student interests into account when developing units of work, creating tasks, and designing assignments?
- Are classroom teachers aware that some students find the content uninteresting? Do they attempt to compensate for this fact by embedding the content in activities, tasks, and assignments that engage students who are not interested in the subject?
- If student interest in the subject or content is low, are teachers more attentive to designing high-interest activities than when student interest in the content is high?
- Are curriculum materials available that will support students' working on and with the concepts, facts, skills, understandings, and other forms of knowledge it is expected they will deal with, understand, and master?
- Do teachers employ a wide range of media and presentation formats to appeal to students with different learning styles and ways of thinking?
- Are electronic technologies viewed more as learning technologies than as instructional technologies?
- Is the content that is presented rich? That is, as much as is possible and practical, are students called on to conduct experiments, read primary source materials, and read books and articles that convey powerful ideas in powerful ways?
- When students are assigned to read a book, use a computer, or employ some other means to acquire information, do teachers ensure that students have the skills to use these technologies?
- When discussions occur, are they disciplined with facts and the rules of logic?
- Are serious efforts made to cause students to use what they are learning to analyze problems, issues, and matters of concern to them?
- Are serious efforts made to encourage students to develop an interdisciplinary perspective—for example, to see how what they are learning in a history class might have relevance for what they are learning in mathematics, language arts, and other subjects?

Standard 5: Product Focus

- Do teachers systematically assess students' interests to determine the kinds of products that will be of interest to the students?

- Is the work teachers assign always linked to a product, performance, or exhibition? Do the products, performances, or exhibitions clearly form a connection among twenty-first-century skills, required concepts and knowledge, and the basic skills all students need to learn and use?

- Do students see a clear connection between what they are doing and what they are expected to produce?

- Do teachers endeavor to personalize products so that different student interests are responded to while students are engaged in what is otherwise the same activity? For example, are students who have a high need for affiliation accommodated at the same time that those with a strong need for independence and novelty are accommodated and responded to?

- Do students generally place personal value on the products and performances they are asked to produce?

Standard 6: Clear and Compelling Standards

- Do students clearly understand the standards by which their performances, products, and exhibitions will be assessed?

- Do students find the standards used to assess their work relevant, meaningful, and important? Or do they view these standards as personally irrelevant conditions they must meet to satisfy the needs of the teacher or the system?

- Are students encouraged to assess their own work in terms of the standards set, and do they participate frequently in group assessment processes?

- Do teachers routinely hold assessment conferences with individual students or small groups of students for the purpose of assessing the quality of student products?

- Is student success in creating a product that meets the specified standard the primary goal of assessment, or is the goal of assessment to justify the distribution of rewards and grades?

- Is timeliness treated as a condition of work rather than as a goal or a standard? For example, do teachers place more emphasis on the quality of the product than they place on the amount of time required to produce it?

- Are peer evaluation and public discussions of performances, exhibitions, and products commonplace in the classroom and in the rest of the school?

Standard 7: A Safe Environment

- Are the school and each classroom objectively safe environments? For example, are there significant numbers of discipline referrals, acts of violence, and threatening behavior?
- Do students and teachers feel that they are as safe as they can be in the school?
- Do the faculty and the administration treat each other with respect and deference? For example, are conversations and discussions in the teachers' lounge and faculty meetings friendly and civil, or are they characterized more by hostility, snide remarks, and generally discourteous behavior?
- Do faculty members treat students with respect?
- Are students respectful of each other and all adults in the school?
- Are student interactions (for example, in peer evaluations) respectful, friendly, and supportive?
- When students fail to meet standards but are making sincere efforts, do the teacher and the student accept the failure as a normal part of the learning process? Or does the teacher respond to nearly all failures to meet standards with negative comments and sanctions?
- When failures occur, does the teacher or do other adults work directly with the student to diagnose the cause of the failure and correct the situation?
- When a student (or group of students) fails to meet standards after numerous tries, do faculty members work together to find new approaches to the task?
- Are sincere efforts being made to ensure that students have access to the resources needed (people, time, and technologies, in particular) to provide optimum opportunities for success?

Standard 8: Affirmation

- Are students, individually and in groups, provided opportunities to display for others what they are doing in class and during the rest of school? For example, are sixth-grade students writing stories for second graders?

- Are parents and guardians invited into the standard-setting process for students, and do they function as full partners in the evaluation of students' performance in school and particularly in the classroom?

- Do adults other than parents, teachers, and guardians regularly view student performances and products and comment on what they see?

- Is the work students are assigned designed in a way that clearly communicates that the effort each student expends is important not only to his or her learning and to himself or herself but also to the functioning of the group and the needs of others who are significant to the student?

Standard 9: Affiliation

- Does classroom and out-of-classroom work often involve two or more students working together on a common product?

- Is group work designed in such a way that cooperative action is needed to complete the work assigned successfully, or could the work be accomplished by one person working alone?

- Are students frequently given work to do that requires them to work with parents and other adults in the community (including senior citizens) to complete tasks and assignments?

- Are some of the products students produce clearly intended to be useful to other students, parents, or community leaders?

- Do students know enough about group processes to analyze and evaluate the operation of their own groups?

- Is electronic technology used to build cooperative networks among students, as well as between students and adult groups?

Standard 10: Novelty and Variety

- Do teachers employ a wide range of formats and varied modes of presentation?

- Are all students provided opportunities to lead others, and are they offered assistance in carrying out leadership functions when they have difficulty?

- Is the setting for instruction varied, or does all instruction occur in a classroom?

Standard 11: Choice

- Are students provided opportunities to select modes of presentation and means of acquiring information?

- Are students provided opportunities to participate in decisions regarding the processes to be employed in assessing performance and determining the standards by which their performance will be evaluated?

- Are the technologies available to teachers and students varied, ranging from pencils to sophisticated computer programs, presentation technologies, desktop publishing, and so on?

- Do teachers and students know how to use the technologies available to them, and is easy access ensured?

- Do students and teachers feel that they have significant control over their own destiny in the classroom and the rest of the school, or do they feel relatively powerless?

Standard 12: Authenticity

- Does the quality of products, performances, and exhibitions have consequences for the student? Does the student care about these?

- Do students feel that the tasks they are assigned are within reach if they expend the effort?

- Are tasks designed in ways that increase student ownership for the quality of the results?

- Are the consequences of meeting, and failing to meet, standards taken into account in the social calculus by which peer groups assign status and provide honor and support?

- Is the work students are assigned designed in such a way that students have a positive stake in, and care about, the success of other students? Or is the work designed to make the success of one student a contributor to the failure of another (such as grading on the curve)?

STARTING THE CONVERSATION

There is no single prescription for the way the needed dialogues might occur in a school or within the private reflections of individual teachers. I am persuaded, however, that unless such dialogues do occur, and on a systematic basis, there is little chance that the power of Working on the Work can be fully realized.

One way a faculty might begin this process is each month to take up one of the dialogue topics in the Working on the Work vision and its related questions and assign responsibility to different faculty members, or teams of faculty members, for developing a data-based answer to each of the questions listed. Each question focuses attention on a slightly different dimension of the same set of issues. It is only when these issues are fully illuminated that a faculty, or an individual teacher, is in a position to design work for students and design schools that support that work. Such a collective view is essential if useful school improvement plans are to be developed. The scheduled faculty meeting could provide a forum for reporting on conclusions, discussing their accuracy, and considering possible implications for action. If professional learning communities have been established, these structures might be used as well.

Another way a faculty might proceed is for each faculty member to set out the questions into a questionnaire format and then use a summary of responses to these questionnaires as the basis for faculty discussion. The intent of the conversation should be to reveal areas of both consensus and disagreement and seek consensus based on arguments that can be supported by data. Distributions of responses are most useful in the pursuit of such a goal. It would be a mistake, therefore, to report responses in the form of mean scores. The distribution of responses will be more useful.

Individual teachers, perhaps using the content of this chapter as a guide, could set about systematically examining the operation of their own classroom. In the course of this examination, they might want to interview students or perhaps develop and administer a questionnaire to students.

Some teachers may be uncomfortable with such crude measures; nevertheless, they are better than no measures at all. Over time, the measurements can be refined, but nothing can be controlled that cannot be measured, and nothing can be measured that is not understood. Understanding, measurement, and control of critical processes are the keys to improvement. As understanding deepens, the need for more precise measures will increase. I have no doubt that the inventive capacity of educators will be sufficient to create what will be needed.

In support of this end, individual teachers might want to supplement their own observations by inviting trusted colleagues and the principal to act as critical friends, with the focus of the critique being on the perceived accuracy of the teachers' descriptions of their current reality rather than the quality of the work being done by each teacher. (Too often we evaluate and try to improve things before we fully understand them. Sound description should always precede analysis, and analysis should always precede evaluation.)

THE ISSUE OF TIME

Activities like those described in this chapter can be time-consuming. It may sometimes be necessary, for example, to hold a one- or two-day faculty retreat in which the entire agenda is committed to ensuring a careful assessment of one or more of the sets of questions listed in this chapter. What is important is that the principal and teachers have some confidence that they have given consideration to the issues associated with each of these questions. It is the obligation of school leaders to ensure that the issue is addressed. For example, assume that an elementary school principal, as a result of conversations with students and with teachers, becomes persuaded that students are not spending much time in the study of science, and much that they are taught in the name of science is inaccurate, shallow, or otherwise suspect. Furthermore, this condition is not confined to a single classroom or to one teacher. Among the actions the principal might take are these:

- Engage the faculty in a conversation regarding the science curriculum and what they believe students need to know and be able to do at what levels.

- Encourage faculty members to compare what they say they believe children should learn to official mandates.

- When there are discrepancies between what faculty members say and the official mandates, encourage discussion of why these disagreements exist. It may be, for example, that the reason for the discrepancies is that faculty members have never been informed about the official expectations, or they have been informed but do not find these expectations either compelling or binding.

- Given the results of this discussion, encourage the faculty to work together to create a solution to the problems identified. For example, if the root of the problem seems to be that teachers have had little exposure to science, then the faculty might want to work with a high school science department to create a summer science workshop for teachers and find ways to get high school science teachers to provide ongoing support to them as they work toward strengthening their background in science.

The most critical thing to remember is that the questions outlined in this chapter are intended to provide a discipline from which principals and teachers can carry on a reasonable discourse regarding the intentions of the school faculty and the relationship between those intentions and the desires of parents and communities. Such disciplined conversations are needed if reflective discussions are to increase and meaningless babble and "happy talk" are to decrease.

Prototypes and Design Specifications

After reflecting on some common concerns they were having in getting their fourth graders to invest time and energy in their math assignments, a group of fourth-grade teachers decided to jointly design a mathematics unit. One of the teachers volunteered to offer his students as the target group of learners. The group worked with him using questions so all of them were clear about what he knew about the group's motives and which design qualities would be key in whatever they designed. They agreed that they would use the design process to create a prototype that they could eventually use by making necessary changes based on different groups of students, different sets of needs and interests, and perhaps different design qualities—design specifications—to be emphasized. The group carefully thought together about Standard 3: Content and Substance, which they wished to address, recognizing that what they wanted students to learn was one of the design specifications. Next, the group considered what products, performances, and exhibitions might best be required of students in order to cause them to learn what the teachers intended.

Before they plunged in and used the design specifications to generate learning experiences, the team summarized the specifications for themselves, along with the design challenges they faced addressing one teacher's specific students.

When teachers prepare to design work that engages students, they must begin by identifying the motives and values students bring to their work. Then the individual teacher designer, usually working with colleagues, can begin to imagine ways of linking these motives and values to work that has characteristics most likely to be responsive to those things about which the students care. At the same time, the designer must ensure that the successful completion of the work will require students to learn what the teacher intended.

PROTOTYPES AND PROTOTYPING

Prototypes and prototyping are prominent ideas among designers. These ideas are also useful in the effort to understand the process of designing work for students. At the most basic level, prototypes are early examples of a proposed solution to a design problem. For teacher designers, the design problem is to create work that is engaging and results in profound learning, done within the context of agreed-on curriculum standards.[1]

Prototypes are not models. Rather, they are ideas expressed in a concrete form that can be made available to others for comment and for evaluation. Prototypes are disciplined by research, but they are just as often the result of inspiration, intuition, and creative insight as they are the result of research.

Prototypes begin with a set of design specifications that clearly indicate what the product is supposed to do and what essential features it should have. For example, designers of laptop computers will likely be attentive to battery life, an important design feature of concern to many potential customers, and they also are likely to be concerned about the weight of the computer. So when they set out to design a new computer, the design team will adopt some clear specifications

---

[1]This is not necessarily an endorsement of the idea of national standards. Rather, it is an acknowledgment of the obvious fact that one of the functions of schools is to ensure that students learn those things they need to know and that teachers, parents, and other members of the community must become clear regarding what those things are. The last chapter of this book turns to a discussion of the idea of standards and accountability.

with regard to these matters—for example, that battery life should be at least four hours and the weight should not exceed five pounds.

After identifying and specifying the relevant elements, the designers begin to imagine a product or solution that will meet the design specifications. There are few rules to follow in design other than to begin with the customers' needs and values and develop product specifications that honor these needs and values. Based on their insight into the needs of their customers or clients, designers begin to construct a vision of a product that will satisfy the requirements.

Once the vision of the product becomes clear, it is common to develop a concrete model that is thought to express all the qualities the design specifications call for. Included in the design are the kinds of materials and technologies it will take to construct the product in a reproducible form. Sometimes the initial version of this product will be nothing more (or less) than a written document or a graphic presentation, but eventually the prototype evolves into a concrete and operational example of the product.

Of course, designers consult whatever research is available, but the source of the design could be a provocative metaphor as much as a brilliant research piece. The prototype is not valued because it is consistent with the research; it is valued because it responds to the needs of the clients and is not contraindicated by whatever research is available

Often the first test of a prototype is a critical review by the team charged with designing the product. Once the design team is satisfied that what they have designed has a prospect of working in the real world, they take the product out for field tests. Based on feedback from the field, they make modifications—sometimes only minor tweaks and sometimes major overhauls.

PROTOTYPING AS A TRANSFORMING DEVICE

The need to transform schools engenders a great deal of discussion today. Unfortunately, many who argue for this use the term *transform* as a synonym for the word *reform*. This is a mistake that can cause considerable mischief to the cause of school improvement.

Reformation leaves the fundamental systems that define behavior inside schools intact. The aim of reform is to make the existing system more effective at doing what it has always been intended to do. In the context of efforts to improve schools, *reform* usually means changing procedures, processes, and technologies with the intent of improving the performance of existing operating systems.

Transformation involves a metamorphosis, that is, a change from one form to an entirely different form. In organizational terms, transformation almost always involves repositioning and reorienting action, either by putting the organization into a new business or adopting a radically different means of doing the work it has traditionally done. Transformation by necessity includes altering the beliefs, values, and meanings (the culture) in which programs are embedded, as well as changing the system of rules, roles, and relationships (the structure) so that the innovations that are needed will be supported rather than rejected. (I address issues more fully related to school transformation in my book *Leading for Learning: How to Transform Schools into Learning Organizations*.)

Translating the design process proposed here into the realities of schools requires the transformation of schools and, especially, the role of teachers. Teachers and those who work with them must change the mental models they use in thinking about their work and the language they use that supports those models. Rather than speaking of learning objectives, they must think in terms of design specifications. Rather than thinking primarily in terms of activities to select, they must think of student motives and student values.

In a transformed school and classroom, learning goals are more important to the teacher than to students. Students are generally more concerned with what they are doing in school than with what they are learning. It is only after they have learned that they begin to impute value to the learning itself, so it is a mistake to think of learning as a motive or a motivator.

Students are seldom motivated by learning itself. Instead, they are motivated to do things. Sometimes those things require them to learn. As I have said before, the genius of school is found in the ability of teachers to design things students want to do that result in students' learning what their teachers and the larger community believe they should learn.

Students in schools focused on engagement want to learn because what the school and teachers encourage them to do provides them with opportunities to satisfy the values they bring with them to the school and their classroom— all of which they have learned and some of which they have learned in school. Learning is what happens when they are motivated and the source of the motives is based in the values and needs of the students.

CREATING DESIGN SPECIFICATIONS

The qualities of the work that are important to students are those that provide students with the possibility of intrinsic rewards—that is, rewards students have learned to value that they can gain only by involvement in the work. The Working on the Work framework is a tool that is intended to center attention on these qualities and attributes.

The ten design qualities constitute a heuristic framework that is suggestive of aspects of schoolwork about which students are likely to have concerns and express values that will affect the motivational value of a task. Just as customers for a computer might be concerned about weight and battery life, students might be concerned about such things as the likelihood that they can succeed in carrying out the tasks required to produce the product. (From this point forward, I use the word *product* to mean physical products, performances, and exhibitions.) Or they might be concerned about what happens if they fail on an initial try, what the product they are expected to produce will look like when it is finished, or how much value their classmates place on the product. Design qualities like clear and compelling standards and protection from adverse consequences for failure are clearly suggestive of the fact that the work designed for students should take these factors into account, just as the need for novelty and variety may be a factor, as might the need for affiliation, authenticity, and choice.

AN IMPORTANT ASIDE

As is probably clear by now, the view of motivation expressed in this book is a bit different from the view that teachers commonly embrace. The following summarizing statements may make my position on this matter clearer:

- I begin with the assumption that motives are things the learner has, such as values, needs, and drives that lead him or her to act.

- Motives are of two sorts: those that exist regardless of culture and context and have their origin in the way human beings are wired, and those that are learned and are dependent on culture and context.

- Motives that exist without reference to social context and culture are usually described as basic needs. Motives that are learned and dependent on culture and context are commonly referred to as social motives.

- All students have motives, so it is a mistake to speak of students as being unmotivated. The issue of concern should be to discover the motives students bring to their work and then to design the work in a way that appeals to these motives.

- With regard to schooling, motivators are embedded in the work that students are expected to do or in the rewards and sanctions extrinsic to the work over which their teacher and other authority figures exercise control.

- Motivators are both intrinsic and extrinsic. Intrinsic motivators are those qualities, characteristics, and attributes of the intended activity that promise to satisfy the motives the learner brings to the work and the tasks and activities associated with the work.

- Intrinsically motivated students find participation in the work assigned inherently responsive to their motives. The work is designed in a way that makes it possible for these students to satisfy their needs and values without reference to motivators external to the work itself.

- Extrinsically motivated students do not find meaning or significance in the activity and tasks they are expected to perform. They must be induced to comply through appeal to rewards and punishments extrinsic to the work itself.

- Social motives and values are of a piece. Motivators for students are those things they have learned to value through interaction with others. Those things that serve to discourage students are those they have learned through interactions with others to avoid because they bring psychic or physical pain or, at a minimum, fail to satisfy values that are important to the student.

- Students vary greatly with regard to the motives they bring to their work. For example, some students have learned to place a high value on affiliation, whereas others devalue it. Some students have learned to enjoy some subjects that others have learned to dislike. Thus, students come to value some forms of activity over others and respond to some types of activity more positively than to others. The Working on the Work framework centers attention on those things students have learned to value and devalue rather than on needs that might induce them to behave in compliant ways.

- Social motives rather than basic needs are at the base of the Working on the Work framework.

- The primary task of teachers is not to motivate students. It is to design work they provide to students or encourage students to undertake in ways that maximize the likelihood that the motives students bring to the work will be responded to and satisfied. The task is also to design the work in a way that minimizes the likelihood that student motives will be frustrated or need to be suppressed.

A DISCIPLINED APPROACH TO DESIGNING SCHOOLWORK

In the years since I wrote *Working on the Work*, members of the staff of the Schlechty Center and I have run many workshops for teachers. I argued in my book *Creating Great Schools: Six Critical Systems at the Heart of Educational Innovation* that some of the design qualities were probably more ubiquitous than were others because there is no way to design good work without giving these qualities specific attention. For example, the purpose of designing work for students is to create experiences in which they come to know things they do not now know and come to be able to do things they would not otherwise be able to do. This has to do with content and substance, and it provides the reason for designing schoolwork in the first place. If content and substance are not attended to, there is no reason to design schoolwork. It is for this reason that curriculum standards are so important to the design of schoolwork. Similarly, product focus is essential to transforming what might otherwise be meaningless activity into work, and it is work rather than activity that provides a sense of purpose and meaning to students.

I continue to believe that some of the design qualities are more likely to force themselves on designers than are others, but I believe the distinction I have been making between what I once called "qualities of context" and "qualities of choice" is a distinction without a difference. In any given context, some of these qualities force themselves on the designer, whereas in other contexts, the failure to attend to these qualities may not even be noticed. For example, protecting students from the adverse consequences for failure may not be important when the nature of the work has a great deal of entertainment value and a culture of trust and mutual support can be assumed. But where trust is lacking or the stakes are high, failure to attend to protecting students from adverse consequences can be a fatal design flaw.

By employing a disciplined approach to the development of design specifications and considering each design quality as a nominee for the status of an indispensable element in the context for which the experience is being designed, I believe the problem I tried to address in my differentiation between qualities of context and qualities of choice can be dealt with. This being the case, I have abandoned the distinction, though I do not think it would be especially harmful if anyone continued to use the old framework. With these matters in mind, we can proceed with the discussion of a disciplined approach to the design of schoolwork.

Product Focus

Designing work for students requires teachers to seek to harmonize the activities they plan with the motives of students. It requires as well that they concern themselves as much with flow and form as with behavioral objectives and items on a test. Figuring out ways to build relationships among the elements of schoolwork that provide intrinsic motivation for students and using these relationships to design work is the heart and soul of designing engaging work.

Engaging work often requires one to participate in activity that is in itself not exciting or even interesting. For example, I will eventually receive the proofs for this book. By the time, the manuscript reaches this stage, I have been over each page many times, and I will frankly be bored with it all. Yet the editor will expect me to read it carefully, and I will have limited latitude in what I can add or delete. My choice has been taken away. The possibility of affirmation awaits, but so does the threat that critics will not respond favorably to what I have done. Clearly I must find writing a book engaging, for I have done it many times. But each time I abhor the tasks I must perform in the final stages. I do these tedious tasks in order to affirm my right to claim the other intrinsic rewards I get from producing a book of which I can be proud.

In the meantime, many members of my staff will have read early drafts of this book, and we will discuss their reactions with me. Later I will bring in a group of teachers and administrators to review the product, again providing collegial support as well as some degree of affirmation of the importance of my contribution to their work. This anticipation keeps me going, even though I know there are many things I will have to do to finish this book that I will really not enjoy.

The kinds of questions that design team members should keep in mind when developing a list of specifications that take product focus into account are as follows:

- Is the nature of the product, performance, or exhibition that is to result from this work clear? If not, at what point will it become clear? Sometimes it is wise to wait to determine what the work product for students will be until the other design specifications have been developed. This is because sometimes the production of certain types of products may preclude the inclusion of design qualities that are perceived to be critical. For example, if the product includes public performances in front of peers, the ability to protect students from potential adverse consequences for failure is greatly diminished. Designers might be well advised in such cases to limit their products to those that guarantee a degree of anonymity and shared responsibility.

- Does working on this product call on students to work with information, skills, and processes in which they have a real interest? If not, what is the rationale for choosing this product?

- If the product is something the student needs to learn to produce, even though the act of doing so is initially threatening and off-putting, are there ways to reduce the threat value? For example, if students are threatened by entering into public debates, perhaps they could be guaranteed anonymity by using technology that makes anonymous responses possible.

Considering questions like these can sensitize designers to the way different types of projects, products, exhibitions, and performances amplify some design qualities while sublimating others. Answers to these types of questions can also be useful in seeing the linkage between and among different types of tasks and how this linkage might best be exploited. For example, students who are reluctant to speak before peers might first be encouraged to prepare scripts for a speech that would later be incorporated into a well-rehearsed video presentation. Once a student has experienced some success with this type of work, he or she might be encouraged to speak more spontaneously.

Content and Substance

Many who teach do so because they find academic work and the study of the subjects they teach personally satisfying and gratifying. Dan Lortie, a well-known sociologist, once said to me, "Teaching does not attract many counter-identifiers," by which he meant that teaching did not attract many people who found schoolwork uninviting.[2] It is nevertheless important that teachers are clear about what they want their students to learn and about the students' disposition toward that knowledge. The following questions are related to content and substance that individual teachers and design team members need to ponder as they set about designing engaging work for students:[3]

- As a result of successfully performing this work, what will students know and be able to do that they do not know and cannot do now?

- Why is it important that they know these things?

- What subjects, content, or skills will students need to master—and at what level—in order to do this work?

- How will we know that students have learned what we intended, and how will we know that what we know is so?

- How do students feel about these subjects and skills? Do they find them intrinsically valuable, or are they disinterested, or maybe even hostile, toward the topics to be considered?

Given answers to these questions, the designers should be able to articulate what students should learn as a result of this work and how they will know if students have learned it. Equally important, they will be in a position to judge how much the content to be taught will serve as a motivator or, if it is not a motivator, to specify how to address this problem. For example, the designers might specify that special attention should be given to enriching the content in ways that students might appreciate, such as through the use of multimedia presentations or dynamic outside speakers.

Organization of Knowledge

The assumptions designers make about the way knowledge is, or should be, organized is a critical element in the design of work. Knowledge can come in

---

[2]Dan Lortie, *School Teacher* (Chicago: University of Chicago Press, 1976), remains one of the best studies of the teaching occupation that has been produced to date.

[3]The questions listed here, as well as in subsequent discussions of the other design qualities, could be used as well in the design of work for teachers or in any other educational setting where the intent is to increase engagement in knowledge work. Here, however, I have limited my discussion to the use of these questions for the design of schoolwork.

prepackaged forms—for example, a textbook, a journal article, a speech, a lecture, or a video presentation—or it can be embedded in experience alone. The work may call on students to repackage or reconstruct the knowledge available, or it may call on them to draw on a variety of sources to create the content they need to master. Sometimes direct instruction may be appropriate; at other times, a problem-solving or discovery approach may be required.

One of the key considerations here is the learning styles that will be involved or addressed. When the intent is to use the way knowledge is organized as a means of inviting student engagement, the knowledge should be organized in ways that respond to the preferred learning styles of the students. If the intent is to encourage students to explore new styles or develop new skills, then the knowledge should be organized in a way that presents a relevant challenge to the students—a challenge to deal with content in a way they have not done before or a challenge to process information using technologies with which they are unfamiliar. For example, students who find no intrinsic value in learning to read or have reading difficulties might be provided with electronic games that require them to read in order to participate and then provided with partners to play with who can read and who will depend on them to read as well. In this way, the power of affiliation is mobilized at the same time that the choice of content enhances the prospect that what the students read will be of interest to them.[4]

Here are some suggested questions designers might ask about organization of knowledge:

- Given the content that is to be mastered and the skills to be developed, what resources are available that bear on the subjects involved? For example, what does a Web search reveal about possible sources of instruction? Are there prepared programs that reveal sensitivity to the need to create materials and approaches that place emphasis on efforts to appeal to intrinsic motives— motives like affirmation and affiliation, for example?

---

[4]I have long believed that for nonreaders, the emotional appeal of the content being read is more important than the substance that might be contained in what they read. Before children can learn to interpret difficult passages in writing (sometimes a boring and tedious task), they must know how to decode words and comprehend written passages. Teaching children to be patient and persist in the face of boredom and humdrum is important, but first let us teach them to enjoy reading. Reading, if it is to be inviting to students, must empower students to do some things they want to do in the here and now. Among the things they want to do is to play video games with their peers and contribute to team success while playing those games.

- Based on experience, what are the types of instructional approaches that students most value, and how might these approaches be honored in the work to be designed?

- Given the nature of the products to be created, what contextual features need to be specified? For example, is group learning to be valued, or should much of the work be done by students who are operating relatively independently?

- Should all the work tasks be done by all these students, or should the tasks be differentiated and assigned to different students depending on their interests in such tasks, their level of understanding of the content, and perhaps their need to develop requisite skills? (Sometimes students should be assigned to carry out tasks that challenge them; at other times they might be assigned tasks they already know how to do in order to facilitate their skills in mentoring others and as a means of affirming the utility of what they know.)

Clear and Compelling Standards

If standards are to serve as sources of motivation, then the students to whom the standards apply must attach intrinsic importance to them. Too often school standards are upheld by a system of extrinsic rewards and punishments rather than by efforts to help students come to embrace the standards as something of inherent value to them. High-stakes testing, for example, is an explicit extrinsic reward strategy, and it suffers from all the weaknesses Pink documents so well in his book *Drive*. Advocates of high-stakes testing often overlook that a much more powerful way of upholding standards is to build the standards into the culture of the school and the classroom. For example, schools and classrooms where excellence is an understood norm are more likely to encourage students to embrace and support challenging standards than are schools and classrooms where the values have to do with minimums and getting by. Schools and classrooms that honor continuous improvement in performance are more likely to make it possible to use standards to motivate than are schools where some pre-specified performance level is announced as the standard to be met to receive a reward. Standards that honor growth, development, and effort are much more intrinsically motivating than are standards that honor only absolute achievement. Working on the culture of the school and the classroom may take longer, but the long-term payoff is almost certain to be better than the short-term gains that might otherwise be made in test scores.

Figuring out how to develop and communicate such standards is one of the major design challenges confronting any teacher who wants to design engaging work for students. Helping students see that effort—as well as ability—influences performance and that high levels of performance can be achieved only by significant effort is also a design challenge.

Indeed, I would argue that one of the fundamental problems in a bureaucratically organized school and classroom is that the students who are most talented are seldom challenged to use their minds as well as they could. Rather, they are challenged to do a lot of work and comply with the rules by which they are to do the work. What they need to learn in order to do the work is relatively minor compared to what they are sometimes required to do to satisfy the demands of the activities with which they are expected to comply.

Less talented students are often required to learn a great deal before they can get any intrinsic or extrinsic reward from what they do. The result is that they feel frustrated and eventually retreat in the face of defeat. Conventional grading practices in schools tend to exacerbate this condition. For example, in a school where an average of 70 is required to receive a passing grade, a student with a 69 needs to improve only one point to move up. The student who has an average of 30 must, relatively speaking, improve much more to receive an equivalent reward—extrinsic though the reward might be.

Here are some examples of the kinds of questions a design team might want to answer about standards:

- Are the standards by which performances and products will be judged sufficiently clear that students can use them in evaluating their own performance as well as in evaluating progress toward producing the intended product?

- Will students find the standards compelling? That is, do the standards represent a level of achievement or accomplishment that the students truly aspire to and believe is possible to attain?

- Do the standards, as they are stated and understood, serve to inspire mastery—getting better and better at something the student believes to be important—or passive acceptance rather than commitment?

Protection from Adverse Consequences for Failure

Schools and classrooms should be places where students are challenged to do things they have never before done and use intellectual tools they have yet to master. This means that students should be encouraged to take the risk of failure. If, however, students are to take such risks, they must be protected from negative consequences when they do fail and they must receive continuous feedback regarding whatever progress they are making. As I wrote earlier, students do not mind failing. What they mind is being punished for it.

This being the case, school should be a place where it is assumed that there will be a great deal of failure, and students should be protected from being embarrassed, humiliated, or otherwise sanctioned simply because they fail to meet a given standard at a given time. This does not mean that standards do not count or that they should be lowered to accommodate those who do not or cannot meet them. Neither does it mean giving A's for effort. What it does mean is that work should be designed so that the standards for the work and the products of the work are built into the work itself and continuous feedback about progress toward meeting those standards is routinely provided.

Does this mean that teachers must grade more papers and check more homework? No! What it means is that teachers, principals, and all who work in and around schools consider ways of designing schools so that the context in which schoolwork is done, in addition to the work itself, provides useful and meaningful feedback regarding what Pink refers to as the drive for mastery, "the desire to get better and better at something that matters."[5]

The first step in protecting students from the adverse consequences of failure is to ensure that the standards by which success and failure in schools and in classrooms are judged are about things that really matter not only to the students but to those to whom students refer for guidance and direction. In other words, if standards are to matter to students, we must first ensure that these standards really matter to the adults who are significant in the lives of students. And who are the people who count for students? For most students, their parents, teachers, and peers count. Federal and state bureaucrats do not count—at least not until students reach high school age, and prior to middle school, only a few students are concerned about what college admissions officers have to say about them.

The power of the peer group in enforcing standards is well documented. Indeed, one of the problems confronting teachers in schools with large minority populations is that some black males see compliance with academic standards as

[5]Daniel H. Pink, *Drive* (New York: Riverhead, 2009).

a violation of standards they uphold, standards that say that to succeed academically is to "act white." Similarly, in some so-called high-performing schools, the competition for the relatively scarce symbols of success (grades and academic honors such as being named valedictorian) is so great that students resort to cheating and endeavor to create other norms by which they can evade the imposition of standards about which they have no personal concern.

Teachers can protect their students from the adverse consequences of failure and encourage risk taking in various ways. The most obvious way is to establish trusting and supportive relationships with students and communicate to students that their teachers are truly concerned about helping them to succeed and want to celebrate their successes with them. (Good coaches do this all the time.) For the most part, however, protecting students from the adverse consequences of failure is dependent on the culture of the school and the policies the school supports regarding matters like grading, evaluation, testing, and the distribution of symbolic rewards, such as the bestowing of honors and special recognition. When matters such as grading are dealt with as a means of communicating with external agencies—for example, colleges—the harm that grades might do can be minimized. However, when grades are used as a basis for labeling students (for example, labeling students as "A students" or as "just C students"), grades become potentially harmful extrinsic rewards that force the talented into compliance and the less talented into accepting the fact that the best they can expect from school is to avoid being labeled a failure. The best protection from failure is to provide many avenues for success and to minimize the extent to which the only standards that really matter are those that can be translated into test scores. Surely the fact that a student can and does read is as important as a test score on a reading test. Surely the fact that a student learns to do well on a reading test but in the process of doing the work required also learns that reading is not a distasteful activity is important too.

Work should bring joy along with the exhilaration that accompanies getting better and better at something that is important. Real work is sometimes hard, but it need not be distasteful and painful. Standards that lead to continuously improved performance promote mastery; these are standards that are far enough out of initial reach to be challenging but close enough to inspire confidence that with effort the standard can be met. (I have more to say on this subject in the final chapter of this book.)

The following are some of the kinds of questions concerning protection from adverse consequences for failure that design team members might want to address:

- Will students who fail be publicly humiliated by failure to perform up to standard, or will failure be construed as just another try?

- Are students encouraged to learn from their failures? For example, is the work designed in a way that students are encouraged to evaluate their own work and spot deficiencies before their teachers or peers note these shortcomings?

- Is the work designed to provide little successes along the way and to limit the prospect of high-stakes failures?

- When students fail, are they encouraged to seek support from peers as well as from their teachers, parents, and others?

- Are the standards sufficiently demanding to present a challenge to the highest-performing students but at the same time sufficiently achievable by students who are less quick or sophisticated?

Affiliation

Too often teachers use affiliation as a reward for good behavior: "If you do what I ask, then I will let you choose those with whom you work." Sometimes isolation from others is used as a punishment. Building affiliation into work is different from using affiliation as an extrinsic reward to induce compliance.

In designing work, affiliation plays a different role when it is to function as an intrinsic motivator rather than as an extrinsic reward. In an environment in which it is seen as an intrinsic reward, collaborative action is a requirement of the work—something that one must do in order to accomplish what needs to be accomplished. Because students, like adults, are often motivated by values that are shared with others (a sense of shared purpose), designing work that requires collaborative action and shared purpose can be a powerful source of intrinsic motivation.

Here are some questions about affiliation that a design team might want to ponder:

- Do the students have the team skills and group skills that might be required if affiliation became a key source of intrinsic motivation?

- Is it possible to design the work in such a way that if group activity is involved, each member of the group will see what he or she is doing as valuable to himself or herself and to other members of the group?

- What has been the prior experience of students with work that required collaboration, and how do they feel about this experience?

- For students who have had negative experiences with group work, what in their view made these experiences bad?

Affirmation

Children, like most adults, like to feel that their presence and involvement count for something, and they want to have this presence affirmed. They want to feel that what they are doing matters to those who are important to them and they need reassurance that this is so. Praise is one way this is accomplished, but praise does not always affirm the student; it may simply reinforce the student and encourage him or her to continue to behave as he or she is now behaving or has behaved in the recent past. Affirmation is more forward looking. It seeks to encourage the student to press on and do better not only for himself or herself but also for others who are dependent on him or her. Affirmation is a response to the drive for mastery, and being affirmed encourages students to pursue mastery.

Getting better and better at something that is important can serve as a motivator only when one can see that one is getting better and that others who are important notice and take it into account in their interactions. The Boy Scouts and Girl Scouts recognize that this is so. It is not uncommon, for example, to have competitions among various "patrols" (a team of scouts) relative to the number of merit badges earned in a given period of time. This encourages scouts who have already attained a merit badge in one area to serve as mentors and coaches to others who are seeking these badges. This affirms the contribution of the master scout to the group as well as encourages neophytes to pursue mastery as a contribution to the group. Moreover, all members of the patrol encourage those who already have some of the merit badges to pursue others because this too is a contribution to the life of the group.

Teachers who are serious about designing engaging work for students should look at organizations like the Boy Scouts, Girl Scouts, Future Farmers of America, and 4-H for inspiration. These organizations are predicated on the assumption that for the most part, students learn by what they do rather than what adults do to and for them. Another source of inspiration might be some of the more sophisticated homeschool networks, where busy parents who want to homeschool their children are provided with illustrations of novel ways of using e-learning opportunities, community resources, other adults, and cross-age study groups to support their efforts.

Many parents who engage in homeschooling quickly discover that for their children to learn what they need to know, the children must be brought to assume considerable responsibility for their own learning. Many homeschool parents, and those with whom these parents consult, work to develop (dare I say *design*) tasks for their children that make it possible for their children to be self-taught and instructed by others rather than be provided routine instruction by the parents. Possible questions a designer might ask about affirmation are

- Have the students been taught about group life, and do they have the collaborative skills needed to benefit from and contribute to work in a group context?

- Do students participate in social networks? If so, what is the nature of these networks, and how do students use them?

- Are students knowledgeable about the way digital tools might be used to support collaborative activity, and are they skilled in using these tools for work-related purposes?

Choice

Students can be provided choice in what they do and what they are required to learn. The power of choice is that it increases the control the student has over the work he or she is expected to undertake. Providing choice is a means of satisfying the drive for autonomy, and as Pink demonstrates, the drive for autonomy is a powerful force with regard to intrinsic motivation. The belief that one is in control, or at least has some influence over one's own destiny and one's own activity is in itself a source of satisfaction. Providing choice is a means of supporting this belief.

When I write and speak of choice, I am not arguing for the idea that every child should be doing his or her "own thing." Frankly, I see such thinking as nonsense. There are some things that students must learn if our culture is to survive; there are some means of doing the job that are better than others. This said, it still makes sense to provide students with as much choice as is possible in what they will need to learn, how they will learn it, and when they will learn it. Moreover, when choice cannot or should not be provided, designers need to recognize that they have framed their design problem in a way that makes it more difficult than would be the case if the drive for autonomy and the motives the drive for autonomy engenders could somehow be responded to.

The following are questions designers might ask regarding issues related to choice:

- Do the students have sufficient mastery of the content to be studied or the skills to be refined that they can be expected to make informed choices regarding the way they should proceed?
- Does the nature of the product permit choices in the content to be studied, or is mastery of the content the primary intent? (For example, if a student is to develop skills in writing persuasive essays, does it make a difference what the subject of the argument is?)

Novelty and Variety

Novelty and variety are particularly powerful forms of motive force, especially when many of the tasks associated with the work are tedious, humdrum, or routine. There are times when a student needs to repeatedly practice a particular skill (learning to write script, for example) or engage in a routine task that presents little inherent challenge and invites little in the way of creativity. (The earlier story about the requirements that authors check galley is an example.)

Given this circumstance the teacher might seek to design the work in such a way that its routine aspects are segmented into short bursts with those aspects of the work most likely to provide intrinsic rewards interspersed. More important, the designer might strive to shape the work so that the relationship between the routine work and the more exciting and intrinsically motivating aspects of it are clear. For example, students often engage in seemingly endless rehearsals for events that will culminate in public performances that others (especially their parents) value. Linking needed routine tasks to public performance is, in fact, one of the most powerful means I have seen to make seemingly meaningless rote learning take on meaning and become therefore engaging work.

Potential questions for design teams to consider in relation to novelty and variety are as follows:

- Have the students developed to the point that they can maintain intellectual work for sustained periods of time?

- Do the students generally get excited about the pursuit of ideas, or do they need to be attracted by unique or novel packaging of the ideas—for example, video games, skits, plays, or student-made video productions?

- Based on prior experience with the students, what kinds of activities are likely to bore them and therefore cause them to seek diversion and distraction?

Authenticity

Authenticity has to do with genuineness. Activities that satisfy the need for authenticity accept the students' definition of the situation as the most important concern and are designed to conform with these definitions. For example, although soccer is "only a game," it provides many students with a sense of identity with teammates and schoolmates. Student needs for status, a sense of space, and a sense of place are often genuinely served by athletic competitions.[6] Activities that respond to the need for authenticity accept the world of students as a resource rather than a problem. The work is designed with an eye toward capitalizing on existing student status systems, existing social networks, and the values of the student subculture. For example, in a school where students are oriented more to athletics than to serious studies, students might be motivated to master subjects in which they are not interested in order to serve as tutors to members of the athletic teams, thereby assisting the team effort.

The following questions are illustrative of those that designers might ask as they make decisions regarding how they will deal with issues related to authenticity:

- What are the qualities and characteristics of those students to whom other students look for leadership and approval? Are they, for example, social stars, star athletes, or outstanding academic performers?

- What is the posture of parents toward the school?

[6]See, for example, Herb Childress, "Seventeen Reasons Why Football Is Better Than High School," *Phi Delta Kappan,* Apr. 1998, 616–619.

- Do parents consistently enforce the pursuit of high performance standards for their children, and are they attentive to reports regarding that performance?
- Are the students participants in nonschool organizations and groups that either reinforce or undermine student engagement in schoolwork?

A CONCLUDING COMMENT

Understanding student motives is key to the design of work that is intrinsically motivating for students. The list of illustrative questions presented in this chapter may seem daunting to those who have not seriously thought about designing the work in which the lessons they devise might make sense. Indeed, it is often assumed that planning lessons is planning schoolwork. It is not. Planning lessons, properly framed, has to do with giving students the tools they need to do schoolwork. Designing work is intended to provide a context in which the lessons taught have meaning and relevance to the students and are therefore more apt to be engaging.

The Working on the Work framework is not a formula. Rather, it is a heuristic device intended to provide suggestions regarding what teachers who want to engage more students more of the time might think about attending to as they design work for their students. The framework is intended to encourage creativity, and it should not be slavishly employed.

An Alternative View of Teaching

Key Ideas

- Batch processing
- Instruction
- Knowledge work
- Mental models
- Platforms for learning
- Platforms for teaching
- Role of student
- Role of teacher
- Technology
- Three types of design teams

A team of middle school teachers has asked their principal to redefine dedicated time for team planning as time for them to become a design team. In order to learn together to become designers, they propose to their principal that over the next six months, they support one another in collaborative design work. In the first few sessions, they want to examine and analyze what makes some of their most successful units appealing to their students. They also intend to review and share a range of digital tools appropriate for their students that could become the source of instruction for future units they design. They want to have a bank of such resources that they can expand and share across their classrooms and various content areas. Then they want to help each other think deeply and comprehensively about the needs and interests of their students so that they will be in a good position to begin some work as designers.

Mental models consist of "deeply ingrained assumptions, generalizations, or even pictures and images that influence how we understand the world and how we take action."[1] The mental models that shape the way teachers view the world of schools have to do primarily with their role as instructors of

---

[1] Peter Senge, *The Fifth Discipline: The Art and Practice of the Learning Organization* (New York: Doubleday, 1990), p. 8.

children. Instruction is, in fact, so central to the role of teachers that the labels *teacher* and *instructor* are often used as synonyms.

It is understandable that this is so. Most of the work of teachers consists of planning instructional activities and carrying out instructional tasks. Indeed, many teachers have received much of their training in college and university departments that carry some derivative of the label "Department of Curriculum and Instruction."

In addition, most teachers see themselves as instructors of particular categories of youngsters and as instructors in particular subjects. Ask a teacher what he or she does, and the odds are that the response will identify the grade level he or she is assigned to teach or the subject specialty he or she claims—for example, "I teach first grade," "I am a middle school teacher," or "I am a high school history teacher." Regardless of the way teachers identify themselves, however, when asked what they do, they eventually come back to one proposition—they instruct children; moreover, they instruct children organized as groups and classes.

In addressing the problems introduced by the need to instruct masses of children, public schools have generally been organized on what could be referred to as the "batch processing" model. For example, all children begin school at the same time of year without attention to developmental differences, and all are expected to progress at about the same rate—thus the concept of "grade-level performance." Consequently, students are typically organized into age-graded classes and are judged to be more or less proficient based on assessments of their performance (usually on standardized tests) relative to test-based grade-level standards.

Generally, schools are organized around the notion that what teachers do in school for the most part they do alone. Of course, schools differ with regard to these matters. Team teaching is, for example, quite common, especially in middle schools, and sometimes teachers, especially in elementary schools, have classroom aides. Regardless of the variants in the configuration of the classroom, however, the central feature of the arrangement is instruction, and central to the instruction is the teacher. Moreover, the instruction is more likely to occur in the context of large groups (fifteen or more students) than in small ones (three to eight students). It is also more likely to proceed on a predetermined schedule than on a schedule that reflects sensitivity to differences between and among students with regard to the rate at which they learn and the time requirements of different forms of instruction.

Because of these structures, instructional techniques are likely to be those that can best be controlled with regard to time allocations and best be delivered simultaneously to large groups. It is, for example, easier to control the length of a lecture than it is to ensure that an intense small group discussion will come to a desired conclusion just as the scheduled time to end the class occurs. Thus, the tradition of lecturing, especially at the high school level, is reinforced by the structure of the school. This structure is often reinforced by the physical layout of the classroom, which may be arranged to make the teacher the central feature in the room.

THE TEACHER'S DILEMMA

Teachers and others who theorize about teaching are well aware that the instruction of children in large groups (larger than eight to ten children) is not ideal and that individual tutoring and instruction in small groups are probably more effective means of instruction. Until the digital age, the economic realities of mass education made—or were perceived to make—such a solution beyond reach. Consequently, educators have spent a great deal of time and energy trying to create ways to individualize and personalize instruction in a context that is designed to support mass instruction and batch processing. The result is that teachers worry much over the fact that the demands of large collections of children gathered in a single place for instruction make it very difficult for teachers to do many of the things they believe are important to educate each child—for example, to coach and assess each child each day in a careful manner. A teacher once said to me, "There are so many of them and so few of me. Their learning styles differ, and I try to adjust what I do to meet their styles, but like everybody else, I am limited in what I can do."

As long as teachers believe that they are or should be the primary source of instruction for children in school or out of school, teachers will always be confronted with this very real dilemma. Fortunately the revolution that has developed around electronic information technologies makes it possible to address the problems this dilemma presents in ways that were not possible in the past.

THE MEANS OF DOING THE JOB

As I use the term, *technology* is "the means of getting the job done, whatever the means and the job happen to be."[2] At the time America's system of mass

[2]See Robert S. Dreeben, *The Nature of Teaching: Schools and the Work of Teachers* (Glenview, Ill.: Scott, Foresman, 1970), p. 83.

education was being formed, learning technologies were quite limited, and the options available to teachers and students were limited as well. The primary means of doing the job was teacher-driven instruction (lectures, mini-lectures, teacher-led discussions, and, less frequently, Socratic dialogues and laboratory experiences) supported by textbooks, workbooks, and limited audiovisual materials, including the ubiquitous chalkboard. Nearly all of this technology was under the control of the teacher or other school authorities. For the most part, neither students nor parents had access to most of these technologies without the involvement of the teacher or other school officials.

Many of these technologies were also at odds with the way students learn. For example, although it is generally well understood that active student involvement and experimentation are essential components in learning, the means most educators used to instruct students often required passivity more than active involvement. In the traditional classroom, students were not encouraged to create content and experiment with different configurations and uses of what they were taught. Rather, they were expected to master and uncritically accept whatever knowledge the teacher transmitted in whatever form the teacher—and school officials—deemed to fit the time constraints and organizational demands of the prevailing system. And because the technologies were faulty, the systems that grew up to support these technologies were misshapen as well. As Seymour Papert, a world-renowned expert in the uses of computers to enhance human learning, puts the case:

> I think that to put this in perspective we should recognize that school has developed a very particular approach to learning. A child starts learning from day one. The learning is driven internally. It comes from personal interest. It is often passionate. It is not cut up into fragments. There is a long list of ways children learn. You can see creative adults doing this too. At the MIT Media Lab you see this, or any research lab, music studio or creative business enterprise—people are learning what they need to know in order to carry things out. That is much more like the way a pre-school child learns. School developed a particular artificial way of learning at a stage where knowledge technologies probably made it impossible to do it any other way.[3]

[3]David S. Bennahum, "School's Out? A Conversation with Seymour Papert," *MEME* 2.13, http://memex.org/meme2–13.html.

Technological developments in the areas of electronic processing, storing, transmitting, and retrieving knowledge and information have opened up new opportunities for learning. To seize these opportunities, however, the rules, roles, and relationships (social structure) that define schools, as well as the beliefs, values, and meanings (culture) in which these structures are embedded, must be transformed—and chief among the things that must be transformed is the role of the teacher. Rather than being viewed as platforms from which knowledge can be distributed, schools and classrooms will need to be thought of as platforms that support students as they work on and with knowledge. In other words, schools and classrooms need to become platforms for learning as opposed to platforms for teaching. Teachers need to involve students in packaging and repackaging knowledge and information in order to make it their own rather than presenting the knowledge to them in a prepackaged and contrived form, as is now so often the case. Teachers need to view themselves as leaders in a knowledge work system rather than as authorities in a bureaucratically organized production system.

Papert summarized well the nature of these changes when he responded to a question about whether teachers will be needed in the future:

> Yes. Will these teachers be people who are in a privileged position as the ones who know and the source of knowledge? I do not think so. Not at all. They will have a very different role. Sensitive well-informed adults who understand deeply about learning processes and social interactions will be able to give advice. They will be able to spot that this kid has a problem, or this kid needs more interesting challenges, or put pressure on them and make suggestions.[4]

THE NATURE OF WORK

Too often teachers confuse work with activity. They assume that if students are involved in the activities that they or the school provides for them, these students are working. This is not so. Work certainly involves activity, but it is more than that. Work organizes activity and coordinates and gives meaning to it. Activity outside the context of work is likely to be without focus or meaning. Work focuses human effort and activity on producing some outcome, performance, exhibition, or product. Work is purposeful activity that has a clear end in view.

[4]Ibid.

In schools, the primary mode of work is what Peter Drucker referred to as knowledge work—that is, working with and on ideas, propositions, symbols, theories, and products that require this type of work.[5] The Working on the Work framework assumes that designing work for students is knowledge work. Their product is work for students that has been designed in ways that are intended to result in optimal levels of engagement. The result is that the role of the teacher as instructor becomes less dominant and the roles of teacher as designer of knowledge work and guide to instruction become more dominant. (I present a much more elaborate discussion of the structure of teacher roles in *Leading for Learning.*) Rather than instructing students, the primary job of the teacher is to design work that leads students to seek instruction and then guide them to the most useful sources of instruction for them.

STUDENTS AS KNOWLEDGE WORKERS

Redefining the role of teachers also requires redefining the role of students. As neophytes in the world of knowledge work, students will be expected to become increasingly independent in their quest for knowledge and in their shaping of tasks that lead them to that knowledge. Rather than providing a platform from which teachers teach, schools and classrooms need to be platforms for learning—both student learning and the learning of teachers and parents. The primary indicators of the success of teachers and schools will be found in measures of profound learning and the development of the twenty-first-century skills that result from doing knowledge work that students find to be engaging and requires them to learn the things they need to succeed.

In today's system, a good student is too often defined as someone who is intrinsically motivated by schoolwork designed to require students to do knowledge work in the manner that academics do it. Academic work, however, is only one form of knowledge work, and it is not the only kind of intellectual work that results in the mastery of academic subjects. Knowing how to create art and music, solve problems, envision new solutions to problems, and reframe problems is not limited to academics or the academic way of doing work.

[5]See, for example, Peter F. Drucker, *The Essential Drucker: The Best of Sixty Years of Peter Drucker's Essential Writings on Management* (New York: HarperCollins, 2001).

If we want more students to be more engaged and more intrinsically motivated to learn academic subjects and see how mastery of those subjects can help them do things they care about, we need to design schoolwork differently. We need to honor many forms of intellectual work that currently are not honored in the narrow definition of what matters in school. Some schools are, for example, moving toward what is called project-based learning, which involves students who create products that require them to apply what they learn and usually require them to work collaboratively. Though this not a new idea—it traces back to at least the 1920s—the presence of new technologies makes the prospects of such an approach much more appealing and attractive to teachers as well as to students. Similarly, some of the more sophisticated vocational education models place increasing emphasis on ensuring that students develop academic understandings at the same time they are developing vocational skills. Certainly we have a better chance of redesigning the work we provide to students than we do of redesigning children, their parents, or the environment from which the children come.

DESIGN TEAMS

If engagement is to become widespread, designing engaging work must become the central task of teachers. As it is now, however, teachers are more likely to be encouraged to think of themselves as planners and performers than as designers and leaders. Rather than designing work for students, many teachers spend most of their time planning random activities for students that they believe will increase the likelihood of improved test scores and then seeking ways to get students to comply with the requirements of the task. Compliance rather than engagement is too often the goal.

It is, in fact, too much to expect an individual teacher working alone to fully exploit the power of design in his or her classroom. The systematic design of engaging work, as well as the design of social systems in which students and teachers do this work, requires a team effort. For this reason, I have come to advocate that school faculties as well as school district officials create design teams. These teams serve as the foundation from which efforts to improve the quality of student experiences can proceed; they also become foundational elements in transforming schools and school districts into the learning organizations they must be if the creation of engaging work is to become a habitual way of doing things as opposed to sporadic episodes in the life of the school.

At the Schlechty Center we think of design teams in three distinct ways:

- District-level design teams focus on developing the capacity of the entire school district to support innovations that increase the prospect of providing students with engaging work.

- Building-level design teams fasten attention on designing systems that support teachers, students, parents, and other members of the school community in their efforts to design engaging work for students.

- The third kind of design team centers attention specifically on the design of engaging work for students.

I will have much less to say here about the first two types than I will about work design teams, other than to say that district-level and building-level design teams are more likely to have a stable membership, whereas work design teams are likely to be more ad hoc and temporary. The reason this is so is that their different types of functions require different conditions in order to work.

Building-level and district-level design teams operate more like R&D units than like school improvement teams. Because this is so, those who are chosen as members are perceived to be especially creative and imaginative or because they provide a needed perspective on the systems that are the subject of the transformative activities that are intended. They are not representative of constituencies. Rather, they are the key intellectual leaders in the school and in the district.

In some ways these teams operate like what Richard DuFour and others call professional learning communities.[6] The difference is that what these groups are charged to learn about are the systems that shape behavior in schools and in school districts and the way those systems affect the capacity to design, plan, and implement significant innovations. Based on what they learn, these teams design prototypes of the kind of organizational changes they believe would contribute to the capacity of the district and the schools to support and sustain the continuous development of increasingly engaging work for students.

Teams that are committed to the design of engaging work are usually established for a more specific purpose, such as designing a unit of work that will result

[6]See, for example, Richard DuFour, "Schools as Learning Communities," *Educational Leadership*, 2004, *61*(8), 6.

in students' learning what they need to know in order to master concepts that have been identified as difficult to teach and hard to learn. For example, teachers and administrators in the Fife School District in Washington State are given mini-grants to support their efforts to design work that addresses what they have identified as difficult-to-teach and hard-to-learn content. (Illustrations of their work can be found at www.fifeschools.com.) Sometimes these teams consist of only two teachers from the same school and even the same grade level, and they may concentrate on designing work that will be especially engaging for a certain segment of the students in a classroom. Sometimes they are organized across grade level and across subjects. Indeed, some of the most productive work design teams I have observed included high school teachers, elementary school teachers, and sometimes students as well.

DESIGN TEAMS AND PROFESSIONAL LEARNING COMMUNITIES

The idea of professional learning communities (PLCs) has become something of a movement in public schools. School leaders who have invested heavily in the creation of these PLCs sometimes try to use these structures as the basis for design teams. Under the right circumstances, this can make some sense. There are, however, some differences between design teams and professional learning communities as they typically operate in schools, and I think it is important to note these here:

- PLCs fasten attention on issues related to the planning of instruction and the assessment of instructional effects. Design teams fasten attention on the characteristics of the work teachers provide to students and seek to learn about ways of increasing the power of this work to engage students. Professional communities could do this, and some do, but for the most part this is not their focus.

- Building-level and district-level design teams fasten attention on system properties and the changes needed in these systems to develop the capacity of the organization to encourage and support continuous innovation.

- The language of PLCs in schools tends to be derived from the fields of curriculum and instruction and from psychometrics. The language used in design teams is systems language and language that facilitates the discussion of issues related to intrinsic motivation (for example, the language embedded in the Working on the Work framework).

- District-level and building-level design teams do not concern themselves with operations or planning; rather, they are concerned with design. This means that they are concerned first with imagining how systems can be designed and redesigned to increase the capacity of these systems to support continuous innovation and to encourage teachers. Then they are concerned with making their thinking regarding these matters available as prototypes (see Chapter Five) to be considered by those who are empowered to act on these systems.

- Design teams concerned with designing engaging work for students develop prototypical units of work that serve as a basis on which members plan activities that are consistent with the prototype and responsive to the needs of specific students. These teams are especially concerned with creating products, performances, and exhibitions that call on students to learn what is intended.

- Typically building-level design teams and district-level design teams have a relatively clear membership roster. Their members have been designated by the principal or the superintendent, usually in consultation with staff and faculty.

THE DESIGN PROCESS

Planning lessons begins with learning goals, objectives, and intended learning experiences. Design begins with students and the specification of what must be built into the work they are assigned or encouraged to undertake if they are to find the experiences provided to be engaging. Design should precede planning, though the demands of bureaucracies often relegate design to a minor role and emphasize planning instead.

The intent of the Working on the Work framework is to serve as a heuristic device that suggests areas of concern in developing design specifications for the creation of engaging work. In the framework, for example, instructional goals and objectives are subsumed under Standard 3: Content and Substance, and learning intentions must always be specified. Similarly, the idea of clear and compelling standards suggests that not only must standards be clear, but they must also be communicated in a way that is compelling to students. Indeed, standards that are not compelling have little power as sources of intrinsic motivation; their only function will be one of supporting external control.

Thus it should be clear that learning intentions are important in the design process, just as they are in the planning process, but these intentions fulfill a different function in design than they do in planning. In the planning process, learning outcomes are stated as goals. In design, learning intentions and the experiences they suggest are specifications that set some of the conditions that must be satisfied if the work is to be likely to engage students.

If the design process is to proceed in a disciplined way, however, it must consider matters suggested by each of the other design qualities as well. The first activity of a work design team, therefore, is to settle on these specifications and articulate them as clearly as possible. Once these design specifications have been identified, the next step is to imagine, identify, or create a product or set of products, exhibitions, and performances that will be likely to require students to learn what it is intended that they learn and at the intended level. This includes identifying the kinds of learning experiences that need to be present, the form the instruction might take, and the way all of these matters relate to each other and to the students as well.

At this point, the team might begin to build or identify prototypical learning experiences that satisfy the conditions set forth in the design specifications. For example, if the students to be addressed have had bad experiences in the past when they tried to deal with the subject at hand, they likely will need a great deal of frequent affirmation about the significance of their effort. They will probably also need considerable protection from punishment for failures when they do invest effort. The design challenge is to figure out how the work can be designed to provide these things. The following extended illustration is just one example.

Some years back, a teacher with whom I was working confronted the not uncommon problem that many of her students were prone to the overuse of dead verbs (words like *am, have, be,* and *are*) in writing without consideration of what they were doing or why. Moreover, many of the students didn't care much about the issue.

She set a learning goal of making students more sensitive to the impact that the use dead verbs can have on written prose and ensuring that they could recognize these problems. Here is what she did:

1. She constructed a cardboard tombstone on which students could attach sticky notes.

2. She organized her class into six groups of five students.

3. Each group was assigned the task of reading the local newspaper each day, and each student was permitted to read one additional publication (including

comic books and magazines). These six items were to be the resources the group used in their search for what the teacher called "dead verbs."

4. Every week each team was to identify passive expressions in their publications and list these expressions on sticky notes to attach to their "tombstone."

5. After about three weeks, she told the class that their work was to culminate in two things. First, each group was to write a eulogy in praise of dead verbs. Moreover, they should model the eulogy on a great one from the past. (There are many available on the Internet. All one has to do to locate them is to use Google and the key words *great eulogies*.)

6. The students held a funeral on the school grounds at the end of the six weeks, and each group presented its eulogy.

7. Finally, each student wrote a brief description of the major contribution each member of his or her group made to the work.

Many other teachers have designed similar units of work. Indeed, a Google search using *dead verb funeral* reveals a number of examples reported on the Internet. I do not know if the teacher to whom I refer here originated the design, but I do know that she explained it to me as an example of Working on the Work, and I think she is right in making this claim. Even if her design was not completely original, her use of the Working on the Work framework as a heuristic device inspired her. For example, she knew from the outset that the subject was not engaging for most of her students. In order to get them engaged in an activity where they would become sensitive to dead verbs she needed to find some motive force other than content and substance. She also recognized the importance of affirmation as a motivator to her students. Thus, she required a public display of the "data" students gathered, and each week there was a minor "celebration" for the group that identified the most harmful uses. By requiring each student to select a unique publication to use as a database, each student was expected to make a unique contribution. In this way, she increased the prospect of affirmation as well.

A COINCIDENTAL LESSON

One other point can be illustrated by this example: without a heuristic device like the Working on the Work framework, many teachers seek models to imitate rather than insights that will help them create their own models. More specifically, as the dead verb funeral began to play out in the school, other teachers were so impressed with the level of student enthusiasm and commitment that they wanted to have a funeral in their class and wanted help in adapting the funeral idea to their circumstance. So rather than seeing the funeral as an example that illustrated some principles for designing work, they saw it as a model to adopt or adapt. Many assumed that it was the subject that engaged the students. They did not even think about the possibility that other design qualities—for example, affirmation—might have been involved. Rather than asking what they might learn about designing work for their class, what many teachers wanted to learn was how to design a funeral for a history class, a math class, or a science class.

Even if these teachers were right in their thinking that the novelty of the funeral was the prime motivator, anything gets old. Working on the Work is not about creating a funeral-centered curriculum or any other stock solution. Rather, it is a means of helping teachers think through the design issues they confront when they approach the business of creating engaging work in a disciplined way.

PART THREE

New Roles in Our Schools

The Teacher's Role
Leader, Designer, and Guide to Instruction

Key Ideas

- Designer
- Guide to instruction
- Leader
- Parents as partners

- Relationship between engagement and learning
- Systemic change

After having informal conversations with several colleagues, a veteran teacher thinks that she and some colleagues could do something to become guides to instruction. She begins talking informally with a "band of five" in her wing of an elementary school about how challenging it is to stay current and connected to the lives of students. For example, she quickly admits that she has only a cursory knowledge of useful computer applications available to the school's students for learning at school and from home.

Several conversations later, including a Friday after-school brainstorming session, the group decides that they will help others on the staff think about three categories of student learning resources. First, they will identify age-appropriate computer applications that will not only provide content but also may connect students with others beyond the classroom for learning experiences; second, they will identify community resources, such as art centers, botanical gardens, and local farms, available in a thirty-mile radius of the school, that have materials or resources that might be useful to their students; and finally, they will begin to compile a list of content experts beyond the school who might bring knowledge to students either virtually or in face-to-face experiences—bankers, surgeons, veterinarians, entrepreneurs, youth group leaders, college librarians, local musicians, and the like. Although the band of five is not certain what they will do with their resources, they suspect that they will use the resources, share the resources with the entire faculty, and perhaps partner with some willing parents to codesign beyond-the-classroom experiences for their students.

Teachers are right when they say that many things beyond their control affect student learning. Part of the reason that teachers so often feel out of control stems from the way many schools are organized and led. Theoretically, at least, this situation could be corrected through action by school leaders, up to and including school boards and superintendents (see Chapter Eight). Other factors—for example, the emotional health of the child's family—are beyond the control of educators as a group. Clearly students who have the benefit of supportive parents have advantages. Schools and teachers can influence parents, but parents and the circumstances in which they raise their children are largely beyond the control of teachers or of school officials—and this should be so. The willingness of communities to provide financial support for schools is also beyond the control of teachers, though there is reason to believe that when schools and communities trust their teachers and trust those who run the schools, financial support is more likely to be forthcoming.

These matters aside, the unfortunate fact is that recent state and national school reform initiatives have diminished the extent to which teachers can control things that have a direct impact on the way they do their work—things they must control if they are to center their attention on providing engaging work for students. For example, although the idea of curriculum standards, at least at the district and state levels, is not new, the idea that curriculum standards should be enforced through standardized testing is new. Indeed, scripted programs and state testing programs have reduced teacher discretion so much that many teachers define their work primarily in terms of getting students ready for the test. Some teachers report that they feel free to teach as they believe they should only after the state-mandated test has been administered.[1]

Recent school reform initiatives, especially those that have spun out as a result of No Child Left Behind (NCLB), proceed from a very different set of assumptions about the proper role of teachers and students than does the Working on the Work framework. Many of the assumptions on which this legislation is

---

[1]Linda Perlstein, *Tested: One American School Struggles to Make the Grade* (New York: Holt, 2007).

based are derived from a manufacturing mentality where teachers are viewed as employees accountable to bureaucratic managers and students are products to be shaped and molded in ways that ensure that they meet a specified standard. The Working on the Work framework assumes that teachers are, or should be, leaders, designers, and guides to instruction and that students are, like their teachers, knowledge workers, not products. The assumption undergirding NCLB and, more recently, the so-called Race to the Top are consistent with the notion that schools should be organized as bureaucracies and embedded in the bureaucratic accountability systems typical of government agencies. Indeed, it is increasingly clear that over the past fifty years, our schools have been transformed from community institutions, where it might be possible to create learning organizations, into government agencies where issues of control and standardization become more important than concerns about direction, purpose, and the needs and values of the people being served.

The Working on the Work framework holds that schools need to be organized as learning organizations that provide platforms for students to learn rather than platforms for teachers to instruct and perform. It recognizes that much that happens in school does so because of the unique characteristics of classes of students and the personal attributes of teachers. It assumes that the solution to the problems of schools lies more in helping teachers to create and imagine than in ensuring that they comply with arbitrary rules imposed by bureaucrats far removed from the action.

The result of this contradiction is that teachers often feel conflicted. Many report that while they believe that the Working on the Work framework should guide what they do, the test-score-driven agenda of state and federal bureaucrats compels them to do otherwise. Even worse, many believe, and with reason, that their local school boards and administrators are willing accomplices in imposing these new forms of bureaucratic accountability and are themselves nothing more or less than middle-level functionaries in what is turning out to be a large and complex governmental agency.

I have written extensively about these concerns in *Leading for Learning: How to Transform Schools into Learning Organizations* and have made concrete suggestions in that book as to how they can be addressed. I comment on these matters here only to signal that I am not unaware of the circumstance in which many teachers find themselves. Indeed, when I have been privileged to work with teachers in school systems where top-level leaders have embraced the notion that creating engaging intellectual work for students is the core business of schools (and these have been numerous), it is commonplace for teachers especially experienced teachers, to agree with these comments other teachers have made:

"This is what I came into teaching for!"

"Working on the Work puts the joy back into teaching. (Unfortunately, too many young teachers do not remember many days of joy. They are too busy getting their students ready for the pretest to find out what they need to do to make sure they can pass the state standardized test.)"

"I was going to retire, but now that we are Working on the Work together, I am going to stay around for a while longer."[2]

ENGAGING WORK AND ENGAGING TEACHERS

The words *engaged*, *engagement*, and *engaging* contain complex and subtle meanings. One set of meanings has to do with obligations, duties, and commitments, as in, "She is engaged to be married" or "Her fiancé engaged the services of a minister." Another set has to do with involvement, as in "to draw into, entangle, attract, or hold." And another set, especially attached to the word *engaging*, has to do with pleasantness, winning ways, and charm.

The confusion that can result from these multiple meanings is nowhere as clear as when one uses the words *engagement* and *engaging* in the context of pedagogical discussions. When someone says, for example, that a teacher is engaging, does this mean that the teacher possesses personal qualities that are attractive to students—that is, that the teacher is pleasant, winning, charming, or perhaps even charismatic? Or does it mean that the teacher creates activities for students that draw them in, attract them, hold them, and fasten their attention? Sometimes it seems to mean one of these things, sometimes the other, and sometimes both.

---

[2]These are literal quotes from teachers and they are typical of the responses we get when we interview teachers who have participated in this work. Certainly, we do get some critical responses, the most typical of which is, "There is nothing really new here. Good teachers are already doing this." I agree there is little that is completely new, but this should be the case. After all, I have learned what I know about teaching not only from research and reading but from countless hours of conversation with many teachers. I share the sentiment that Working on the Work is common sense. Unfortunately, common sense is not common practice, especially when one insists on applying common sense in a disciplined way.

Unfortunately, educators too often fail to differentiate between teachers who are engaging as a person or as a performer and teachers who are skilled at providing work and activities that students find engaging. Failure to make this distinction too often leads to the conclusion that the only way to improve education is to work on the performance of teachers. This eventually leads to the hopeless conclusion that the only way to improve schools is to make it possible to recruit more than 3 million college-educated Americans who are personally engaging and willing to provide heroic personal performances on a routine basis for a relatively modest financial reward.

There are, of course, some teachers who, by force of personality, charm, and wit, are able to inspire students to perform even when the subject is difficult or inherently uninteresting. Heroic teachers do exist, but they cannot be the stuff of which great schools are made. There is simply not enough heroic material to go around. What schools need are teachers who know how to routinely create schoolwork that engages students. Schools cannot be made great by great teacher performances. They will be made great only by great student performance.

A more hopeful view would be to accept that people who have the personal qualities needed to hold any audience spellbound for any length of time are in short supply, and persons who by dint of personality can cause others to do things they might not otherwise do are in short supply as well. What is in unlimited supply, once teachers figure out how to design them, are tasks, assignments, and activities that students find engaging and from which students learn those things that teachers and the larger society believe the students should learn.

KNOWING AND TEACHING THE RIGHT STUFF

Teachers who are serious about improving what students learn in school must be just as serious about improving the state of their own intellectual development as they are about their own technical skills. Teachers who read books and talk about them with their colleagues and their students are likely to be imaginative about the work they design for students. Teachers who explore the possibilities of sources of learning in the digital environment are more likely to be inspired to design work that serves the needs and interests of their students.

Teaching is more than a technical undertaking; it is an intellectual and moral undertaking. Those who teach need to have a rich intellectual life of their own if they are to inspire students to pursue academic matters with any amount of seriousness. If the intent of teachers is to be entitled to be viewed as sources of intellectual leadership in a community, then they must behave like intellectual leaders. Intellectual leaders read widely and deeply. Unfortunately the reading habits of many teachers leave much to be desired.[3]

Among the things that teachers who are committed to systematically designing engaging work for students do are the following:

- They join or create study groups where serious books dealing with education issues and contemporary social and political issues are presented and discussed regularly. Kindergarten teachers profit as much from these discussions as do high school teachers. Indeed, I have found that when high school teachers and elementary teachers join the same groups, creativity increases. They read good novels and short stories and listen to music, including the music their students listen to. As Deborah Meier, educator and author of *The Power of Their Ideas,* has said, "And our schools must be laboratories for learning about learning. Only if schools are run as places of reflective experimentation can we teach both children and their teachers simultaneously."[4]

- They explore game-based learning, social networking, and other digital tools that are part of their students' world. They also read and reflect on the ethical issues facing students in the digital environment and adults' increased importance as ethical guides.

- They engage colleagues in serious discussions of the curriculum guide, the content of mandated tests, and other indicators of what the community expects students to know. They then try to figure out what these things say about the prevailing view of what it takes to be an educated person. If they agree with the community view, they say so. If they do not, they enlist the support of colleagues and try to gain political support for their views.

- They work to enrich the dialogue with parents by facilitating the creation of study groups for parents, where members discuss issues of concern and read relevant books.

[3]See, for example, Craig B. Howley, Aimee Howley, and Edwina D. Pendarvis, *Anti-Intellectualism and Talent Development in American Schooling* (New York: Teachers College Press, 1995).

[4]Deborah Meier, *The Power of Their Ideas* (Boston: Beacon Press, 1995), p. 140. See also Kathleen Vail, "Nurturing the Life of the Mind," *American School Board Journal,* Jan. 2001, pp. 19–22.

- They work to be clear about what they believe regarding the ends of education and the purpose of school and engage others in conversations about those beliefs. As many have observed, the ends of education are much broader than the purposes of schools. Too often schooling becomes confused with education, and it is assumed that children who are schooled are also educated. This is not necessarily so.[5]

FOCUS ON ENGAGEMENT AND THE DESIGN OF SCHOOLWORK

The pressure to improve test scores tends to encourage even the most effective teachers to be willing to settle for strategic compliance and hope for engagement. Even in schools with outstanding test scores, especially in suburban middle and high schools, teachers too often settle for strategic compliance; some even accept ritual compliance as good enough. Moreover, many of the programs that are intended to encourage engagement really do not focus on it at all. Rather, they define engagement as active involvement and time on task and pay scant attention to the meaning that activities might have for students.

The signals such activity sends to students, especially to those who generally do well on tests, are potentially quite harmful. For example, providing time to review for the test suggests that what students have learned is of little long-term significance, because the expectation is that students will soon forget it. Teaching test-taking skills can suggest that what you can show is more important than what you know.

Equally unfortunate in schools with low test scores, teachers are often encouraged to seek to increase ritual compliance rather than engagement. Given the press to improve test scores, this response is understandable. Ritual compliance does produce some gains in lower-order skills, and ritual compliance can be produced efficiently through tightly controlled and semicoercive instructional strategies. Unfortunately, such strategies may help students to write brief descriptive paragraphs about poetry, but they will not inspire students to write their own

[5]See, for example, Neil Postman, *The End of Education: Redefining the Value of Schools* (New York: Knopf, 1996). See also Phillip C. Schlechty, *Shaking Up the Schoolhouse* (San Francisco: Jossey-Bass, 2001).

poems or to appreciate in the fullest sense of the word the nature of poems and poetry and what these can do for the expression of human sentiment and feeling.[6]

Certainly test taking and test-taking skills are important. Similarly, well-conceived review sessions are not without merit. The problem comes when scores on tests are considered more important than what students learned and their attitudes toward learning; the result is that much occurs that is distracting to the ends for which schools have been created. Students not only fail to learn what they need to if they are to be considered well educated, but what they do learn is so shallow and vacuous that it may as well serve to lead them astray as to give them a positive direction.

Teachers therefore need to be clear-eyed about the types of involvement that typify their classroom and learn not to confuse strategic compliance with engagement. They must understand as well that ritual compliance has more value as a crowd-control mechanism than it has as a useful tool for producing profound learning outcomes. Teachers also need to be clear about what they expect in terms of engagement as they need to be with regard to expectations for what students will learn. Indeed, these two matters are so interconnected that they can never be fully separated.

Engagement almost always precedes profound learning. Substantial learning is not likely to occur in a classroom where most students are only strategically or ritually compliant or are withdrawing into a retreatist mode. Assessing engagement is therefore a necessary strategy for ensuring the possibility of preventing deficiencies in learning.

Among the things a teacher might do to ensure that he or she focuses on the right things are the following:

- At the end of each day, the teacher can estimate the level and types of engagement in the class and put this information in the form of a pie chart. Over time, he or she can compare these charts to see if there are changes or if patterns emerge.

- From time to time, the teacher might interview students or distribute a questionnaire based on the various descriptors provided in the preceding chapters.

[6]See Linda Perlstein, *Tested: One American School Struggles to Make the Grade* (New York: Holt, 2007).

This process can be a useful tool in helping the teacher see how closely what he or she believes to be the case squares with what students report.

- The teacher could invite the principal and colleagues to help assess the types of engagement that typify his or her classroom and then discuss similarities and differences in the conclusions that the observers reach.

- If the teacher does not like what he or she sees, or does like it and wants to keep it that way, he or she might try relating the patterns of engagement observed to the characteristics and qualities of the work that are the focus of the observation.

TEACHERS AS DESIGNERS

About six years ago, after many members of my staff and I had spent considerable time and effort working with teachers to develop their understanding of the Working on the Work framework, we decided to pull a group of outstanding teachers into a retreat setting to help us better understand how they went about their work. The participating teachers were selected because they had demonstrated unusual proficiency in providing engaging activities for their students. These teachers—about thirty of them—were asked to bring with them a unit of work they had created during the previous two years that they felt was most engaging. They were also invited to bring any artifacts and written materials they thought might be useful in describing to others what they did in the unit.

I was convinced that one of the reasons these teachers were so successful is that they were using the Working on the Work framework or some similar heuristic device of their own invention to design their work. I was wrong. It turns out that what these teachers did was based largely on their intuition. When their intuitive designs matched the motivational frames of their students, the work was engaging. When they missed the mark—and according to self-reports this was quite often—they simply relied on their intuitive sense to design a new unit of work.

Some reported that they sometimes used the framework to help them understand why their intuitively designed units did not prove to be engaging, but for the most part, they did not use the Working on the Work framework or any other heuristic device to discipline the design process. Indeed, as we began to examine the units of work that were presented, it became clear that some teachers used some of the design qualities with great proficiency but didn't even think about the prospect of using others. Moreover, the patterns of use were more a function of the skill set and biases of the teacher than an assessment of the students' motives. Some teachers, for example, were adept at protecting students from negative consequences for failure and providing novelty and variety but seldom thought systematically about ways they might build more authenticity into the work or provide more choice. Few paid much attention to the communication of standards. Those who did tended to think of standards in the form of gatekeepers for access to extrinsic rewards.

The group then began to consider the possibility of using the Working on the Work framework from the outset as a heuristic device to suggest to them areas in which invention might be called for and areas in which activities with particular motivational characteristics might be selected.[7] For example, the participants began to think of discovery learning as a means of enhancing affirmation, and perhaps authenticity, novelty and variety, and other motivational attributes, rather than simply as a means of developing some high-level intellectual skills. They came to understand that some students, especially some high-achieving students, resist pursuing difficult and challenging intellectual tasks for fear they will not score well. They might also worry that this other work will distract them from what they perceive to be their real work: covering as much material as possible and as efficiently as possible so they can get on to the next assignment.

If students are to engage in discovery and the construction of knowledge, as they must do if they are to develop the skills and understanding they need to function well in the twenty-first century, they need some motivation to do so beyond the process of discovery itself. These motivators also must be sufficiently strong to offset the powerful extrinsic rewards that can be more easily gained by simply complying with directives and doing each task assigned without expecting the task to have meaning or value beyond the fact that it has been done.

Indeed, the literature on the American high school, as well as personal experiences and the stories many teachers tell, persuade me that one of the most perverse effects of the existing system of test score accountability is to discourage the most academically talented students from doing the kind of work that will develop the levels of understanding, insight, and skill they will need to negotiate

[7]This, of course, was my initial intent, but my intentions did not come through clearly even to this dedicated group of teachers. A sense of purpose is a result of the way work is designed. Work that is designed in a way that results in the worker having a sense of purpose is likely to elicit more attention and commitment from the worker than will activity designed in a different way.

the world of knowledge work. The extrinsic rewards they, and sometimes their teachers, want are more easily gained by doing meaningless tasks than by engaging in the serious pursuit of knowledge and the construction of meaning. It is much easier to cram for a physics test than it is to do physics.[8] It is much simpler to plan a series of lectures than it is to design a unit of engaging work.

Teachers need not apply the design process I described in Chapter Five to every classroom learning experience. Time and energy would not permit this. Rather, they should apply it systematically as a means of providing the overall architecture that informs the planning of lessons and activities. By ensuring that the content and skills that students will study and, it is hoped, master are clear, and by ensuring that there are clear products, exhibitions, and performances, teachers are in a position to shape the work and the activities so that what students are required to do has meaning and significance to them.

My experience is that as teachers internalize the need to think differently about the motives students bring to their tasks and as they begin to consider how design qualities might appeal to those motives, the culture of the school begins to shift in ways that are supportive of a focus on engagement. It is this shift that ensures that the Working on the Work framework is not simply another program to be installed. Rather, it defines "the way we do things around here."

Another use teachers might make of the Working on the Work framework is to use the questions posed in Chapter Four as a framework for creating a questionnaire or an observation protocol that would help to discipline the conversation between teachers and principals and would serve as well as a means of conversations among teachers. For example, a teacher who is having difficulty getting a high level of engagement in a class might invite colleagues to provide concrete suggestions regarding ways that he or she could increase the presence of one or more of these attributes. Or teachers who have the same students might use the framework as a means of mutually assessing which of the design qualities seem to be most important to their mutual students. The professional learning communities established in many schools might be the ideal vehicle for such disciplined discussions focused on student engagement.

The Working on the Work framework could also be used as a tool to evaluate prospective classroom resource materials—textbooks, Web sites, computer

---

[8]Edward Humes, *School of Dreams: Making the Grade at a Top American High School* (Orlando, Fla.: Harcourt, 2003), provides a story that documents this point.

learning programs, virtual courses, and the like. The descriptors I provided about engagement in Chapter One could serve as the starting point for developing criteria by which to evaluate materials prior to purchasing them.

The Working on the Work framework does provide a discipline, but only if it is used in a disciplined way. Properly used, the framework causes teachers to look beyond themselves and the personal qualities of themselves and their students for explanations regarding why students do and do not do the expected work. My experience, however, has been that when teachers begin to discuss what is going on in the classroom, they quickly revert to talking about what the teacher is doing and the teacher's style and manner of presentation as opposed to the characteristics and qualities of the work the teacher has designed. That this should be so is understandable; most of the conversation about teaching focuses on what teachers do and sometimes on what students do. Seldom is the conversation about what the teacher intends for students to do and why it is assumed that students would voluntarily do such things.

Ritual compliance can be gained through coercion. Strategic compliance can be enhanced through the enrichment of extrinsic rewards. Coercion and the dispensing of extrinsic rewards are available to teachers not because of their expert knowledge or because they have mastered special skills. These are available because they are bestowed by the traditional authority of adults over children and the bureaucratic authority teachers have as the students' superordinate. Engagement requires that teachers have, and exercise, a different type of authority: expert authority that develops out of their deep understanding of student motives and values.

The reason this is so is that engagement occurs only when schoolwork is designed in a way that appeals to values and needs that are real to students. The design qualities identified in the Working on the Work framework reflect some of these values. The framework reflects an effort to codify and make public some of the things that great teachers have always known but may not have had a language to express.

There may be some motivating factors that have been overlooked or looked past by this framework. I am convinced, however, that teachers who use the Working on the Work framework in a disciplined way will find that they increase the number of students who are engaged and the length of time each student is so engaged. When this happens, learning will increase, and the overall performance of schools will improve as well.

TEACHERS AS LEADERS

The idea that teachers are, or should be, leaders is not new. As long ago as 1932, Willard Waller dedicated a large section of his now-classic book, *The Sociology of Teaching*, to a discussion of the teacher as an institutional leader as well as what he called a "personal leader."[9] To be a leader, a teacher must think as leaders do. Rather than asking, "What am I going to do?" leaders ask, "What is it that I am trying to get others to do, and what reasons might they have for doing those things?" Leaders also ask questions like, "How might I link what I want others to do to something those whom I want to follow me want, need, or value?"

Perhaps the most powerful question a teacher can reflect on is, "Would my students be likely to do what I am about to ask them to do if they did not fear negative consequences for failing to do so?" If the answer is no, the best the teacher can hope for is strategic or ritual compliance. Engagement will occur only when the tasks respond in some positive way to students' motives and values. Effective leaders understand this to be so and are constantly identifying and shaping these motive forces. Effective leaders seek commitment; less effective leaders settle for compliance. Effective leaders earn attention; less effective leaders demand attendance. Teachers who understand that students are volunteers and act on what they understand are behaving as effective leaders do.

Great teachers know that students have a limited and truncated view of the world around them and perhaps a distorted view of their own potential and capabilities. As leaders, teachers are obligated to help students move in directions students might initially want to avoid and to cause students to test themselves in circumstances in which they feel uncomfortable and uncertain. Great leaders have empathetic understanding with regard to these matters, but they do not let this understanding preclude them from insisting on more than students sometimes initially believe they can do. It is in this sense that Theodore Sizer's notion of the teacher as coach has more appeal than does the idea of teacher as facilitator.[10] At least this is so for me. But because I also believe that teachers must do more than either coaches or facilitators do, I prefer to use the more generic term *leader* when I discuss the role of teacher.

[9]See Willard Waller, *The Sociology of Teaching* (Hoboken, N.J.: Wiley, 1967). (Originally published 1932)

[10]Theodore Sizer, *Horace's Compromise: The Dilemma of the American High School* (Boston: Houghton Mifflin, 1984).

Teachers, like other leaders, are trying to get others to do things they might not otherwise do: pursue goals they might not otherwise pursue and accomplish things they might not otherwise accomplish. Their special task is to engage students in activities, tasks, assignments, and other undertakings that result in students' learning. Because teachers are leaders, they can learn from other leaders, but because they are teachers, they are also unique, just as other types of leaders are unique.

TEACHERS AS GUIDES TO INSTRUCTION

The third dimension of the role of teacher—guide to instruction—may seem like a minor distinction in the conventional role of teacher, but it is actually a major shift in the role. Teachers have traditionally thought of themselves as instructors, that is, those who provide instruction to others: giving information, providing explanation of concepts, and modeling skills. In the Working on the Work framework, teachers may sometimes instruct but will no longer view instruction as their primary function, because other sources of instruction are available in the time frame of an individual student, not just for the entire class. Other sources of instruction can be available for individuals; they may be synchronized with audio, video, and conferencing potential; and they may serve as a much more compelling source of instruction than any single teacher could hope to be. However, the teacher's overall role is not diminished. In fact, the role of teacher as guide to instruction requires that teachers be "advance explorers" or "scouts" checking out the range of instructional resources available, including guest experts, and become the sources of guidance for students who must learn to evaluate varied sources of instruction for themselves. Finally, in their role as guides to instruction, teachers must be the wise adults who provide guidelines, dialogue, and reflection about the ethical implications of the digital environment our students live and learn in.

TOP DOWN AND BOTTOM UP

"Change where it counts most—in the daily interactions of teachers and students—is the hardest to achieve and the most important."[11] Like David Tyack

[11]David Tyack and Larry Cuban, *Tinkering Toward Utopia: A Century of Public School Reform* (Cambridge, Mass.: Harvard University Press, 1995), p. 10.

and Larry Cuban, the authors of this statement, I am not pessimistic about the prospect of necessary change, but I do worry that failure to advance the cause of school change more rapidly than we were able to do in the twentieth century may lead to the demise of public education as a vital force in America. Moreover, I am persuaded that externally mandated changes are not likely to be sustained beyond the tenure of the individuals who initiated them. Thus, I have little confidence in changes that have their origins in government policies rather than in the genius of local educators. Government policy can serve to inspire local action, but to produce excellence, the policy must not constrain those who will ultimately have to live with the changes that are to be made.

Similarly, top-level administrators, including building principals, cannot make change happen. They can, however, suppress the effects of changes they do not support just as certainly as teachers and community leaders can sabotage any change they do not understand or endorse. That is why systemic change—change that is simultaneously top down and bottom up and touches all the interconnected parts of the organization—is essential.

There is little question that most efforts at change in the past have originated outside the classroom. The failure of such efforts has led some teachers to argue that reforms must come from the bottom up if they are to be effective. That too is a dubious notion. Change initiatives that originate at the bottom will go nowhere if they are not taken into account, supported, and advocated from the top. The role of the teacher cannot change unless the role of the principal changes in complementary ways, and the role of the principal cannot change unless the role of the superintendent changes as well. Most important, change in schools cannot occur as long as the way communities and parents define "real schools" reflects more their longing for the past than their anticipation of the future and all of this is supported by the policy mix of state and federal governments.

It is also imperative that as teachers and schools move toward real reform, faculties and school leaders find ways of ensuring that parents and key community leaders are involved and informed about what is going on and that these people are, and feel that they are, taken into account in any change that occurs. The interrelated roles, perspectives, and commitments described in the next section illustrate what I mean when I say that Working on the Work is a framework, not a program, that requires systemic thinking and change.

FAMILIES AND SCHOOLS

Lack of parental support is a common teacher complaint. This is not a new phenomenon. As long ago as 1932, Willard Waller described the relationship between parents and teachers as fraught with the potential for conflict and feelings (on both sides) that the other party is "letting them down."[12] Changes in the social, economic, and political context in which families exist, plus changes in the structure of families themselves—for example, changes in the size of families, which affects the presence of older siblings who could serve as teachers when they are present—have clearly eroded the capacity of families to help educate their children. This erosion is not the result of intent or lack of commitment and concern on the part of parents. Rather, it is a change in circumstances that has yet to be satisfactorily accommodated in most schools. The following stories about a single family over two generations will illustrate this point:

Act 1: Family Life in the "Good Old Days"

In the 1950s a farmer had a sixteen-year-old son who had just received his driver's license and had arranged his first date. The farmer had mowed hay on Monday and had told his son that they would be taking in the hay and putting it in the haymow on Thursday. The son therefore felt safe in scheduling his date (a trip to the county fair) for Wednesday. On Tuesday morning the farmer woke his son up and told him to get up and out in the field: "We are going to need to take the hay in Wednesday because the weatherman said it is going to rain by Thursday." The son understood the reasonableness of his father's request. He did not complain (although he did grumble a bit) because he knew that what he was being asked to do made an important contribution to the life he enjoyed. His date would have to wait until some other time. A farm girl herself, she understood why the hay was more important than their date.

Act 2: The Price of Mobility and Change

This same son went off to college where he studied to be a veterinarian. He decided that running a small-animal clinic in a suburb held more promise than did large-animal medicine.

[12]See Waller, *The Sociology of Teaching.*

Eventually the son, like his father before him, had a son—and like his father before him, the veterinarian believed in the value of hard work and the need for discipline and sacrifice for goals that are valued. Living in the suburbs, however, he found it hard to come up with equivalents for making hay, milking cows, or doing other forms of work that required his son to develop and demonstrate good work habits. One of the strategies the veterinarian settled on was requiring his son to mow the grass each Wednesday morning, and if it rained, then as soon after Wednesday as possible. (The lawn was large and required nearly all day to complete the chore.)

It turned out that the veterinarian's son was invited to a pool party that was to begin at 11:30 A.M. and last until 5:00 P.M., and yes, dear reader, you guessed it—the day was Wednesday. The father, being a reasonable person, told the son that this one time it would be acceptable to mow the grass on Thursday.

On Tuesday the veterinarian noted that the weather forecast called for rain on Thursday and Friday and his father and mother were coming to town and he wanted the place to look nice. He could, of course, insist that his son forgo the swimming party. After all, that is what his father did when work needed to be done, but somehow he suspected that his son might not view a lawn that looked a bit scraggly the same way he (the farmer's son) had viewed hay that might get wet. Indeed, he suspected that if he insisted his son stay home to mow the grass, his son would see him as being arbitrary and unreasonable. Consequently, he hired a lawn service to mow the lawn, and his son went to the pool party. The son had a good time, but he also learned that the work he did on behalf of his family really wasn't all that important. His father could hire a lawn service instead.

There is much that could be teased out of these two scenarios that might be instructive about the changing role of parents as educators. For example, the problems associated with the effort to translate educational values that have their base in an agrarian world comprising small towns and villages into the more fragmented world of urban America are clear. What may not be so obvious is that the tasks children do around the home today seldom have the educational value that family-based tasks had in the not-too-distant past. Among other things, most of these tasks have no vital connection to the well-being of the family, and they seldom require interdependent work with other family members. In fact, much of the work families have children do today is at least as contrived as is the most meaningless schoolwork. Washing the dishes after dinner (assuming the family has a sit-down dinner and no dishwasher) and mowing the lawn (assuming there is a lawn to mow) do not compare to working side by side with one's parents to plant and tend a garden that will produce vegetables to be canned. Moreover, as our society becomes increasingly a knowledge work society, it becomes more and more difficult for parents to describe, in terms that the children would understand, what they do when they work—and it is nearly impossible for parents to show their children what they do or how they do it.

Yet the fact remains that many of the lessons that families taught and schools depended on them to teach cannot be taught by schools or any other formal organization. They must be taught by those who are much closer to the child than the formal arrangements of schooling make possible. Schools may, for example, develop formal programs of character education, but the fact is that the family and the community, more than the school, mold character. Schools can build on what the family and the community do, but schools are not substitutes for families and communities.

All of these things lead me to what might appear to some to be a simple-minded conclusion: maybe we have the problem wrong. Rather than seeking ways to encourage families to support schools in their educational mission, which now includes doing many of the things that families once did, school leaders might concern themselves with developing the capacity of families to carry out their educational mission in the modern world. Maybe, for example, teachers should concern themselves with helping parents design homework for their children that is really homework—that is, work that can be done only at home but results in learning that is needed and valued in the context of the school. Maybe school leaders should seek ways to help parents develop networks among themselves that provide support to parents in their role as home-based educators, and maybe those who are struggling to homeschool their children should be looked on as potential partners rather than as adversaries. Maybe schools should identify situations where family pathologies are so great that there is no reasonable prospect that the child can receive the family-based education needed and seek to find other ways that this education might be provided—for example, through a strengthened Big Brothers–Big Sisters initiative. There are many examples of such efforts, but in the main, these examples turn out to be the exceptions that prove the rule—the rule being that for the most part, schools provide little support to families or to other agencies that might serve as family surrogates.

Rather than looking to families to enhance the educational capacity of schools, perhaps it is time that teachers and school leaders take it on themselves to enhance the capacity of parents to be the educators they must be if the schools are to work as they should. Students would be better served if, rather than attempting to be surrogates for parents who no longer have the capacity to do for their children what no formal organization can do, teachers worked to strengthen the capacity of schools to support parents to do what only parents and families can do. The following story illustrates what I mean.

A teacher decided that she would use e-mail to communicate with the parents of the students in her first-grade class. (Twenty-three of the twenty-four parents had e-mail accounts.) The student population was diverse. There were parents from inner-city projects and upper-middle-class homes, single mothers who worked outside the home, and traditional families with stay-at-home mothers.

The teacher's view, at least initially, was that parents needed and felt they needed clear communication from her, and she thought that e-mail would facilitate this. It did, but it also fulfilled another need that the teacher had not considered: the need that parents have to network with other parents in their child's class, to converse with them not only about school but about the problems of life in general and the problems of schooling their children in particular.

Such parent networks were present at one time as part of the natural social order in small towns and rural communities. Today parents need guidance in building such networks that will help them understand their own roles as parents in relationship to the schools, their work, and their children.

In the context of this story, discovery of the need for a parent network occurred quite inadvertently. Early on, when the teacher sent parents an e-mail, one or more parents would respond and ask questions or make comments. Some of these parents did not realize that when they hit the Reply All key, all the other parents on the e-mail list would see their response. They soon discovered that this was so and loved it. Indeed, they began to use e-mail more as a tool for parent networking than as a tool to communicate with the teacher or the school.

This discovery led the principal and the faculty to facilitate the creation of support groups led by parents and involving only parents. From time to time, teachers may be invited into these groups as consultants, but the groups are there to build a sense of community among parents rather than to provide a communication link to the schools, much like megachurches use in-home Bible study groups to build a sense of community around the church.

A CONCLUDING OBSERVATION

I have come to believe that one of the most important leadership acts of teachers is to be found in the relationship teachers have with parents. Among other things, they must help parents better understand their role as educators, and they must be prepared to accept the fact that much that we want children to learn cannot be learned in school. Rather they must learn these things at home, in neighborhoods, and in the community at large. Teachers and schools must therefore embrace a new role in which they help to enhance the capacity of parents and communities to provide engaging intellectual experiences for children and youth. Rather than sending schoolwork home and calling it homework, teachers might be better advised to help parents think of ways they can use family-based and home-based experiences to invite their children to learn what the school expects them to learn. For example, I have discovered that my eight-year-old grandson loves to play Monopoly, and he especially likes to play the game with me (affiliation). I am also aware that in the near future, he is going to be presented with math problems that call on him to calculate percentages and to multiply and divide. Monopoly provides many opportunities to prepare him for this schoolwork. Similarly, when I play video games with him, he thinks what we are doing is playing a game; I think what I am doing is providing a reading lesson and building vocabulary. What he does not know is that this is real homework.

Certainly I have advantages over many parents. Not only do I think about these matters all the time, but I have time that many young parents lack. I believe, however, that if teachers positioned themselves as supporters of parents rather than as supplicants asking for parent support, we could help parents see the educational import of much that they do for their children. For instance, they might think about the toys they purchase in terms of the power of the toy to engage the child in important intellectual work. If parents had the support they need, they too might begin to work on the work they give their children, and this would make the work of teachers so much easier.

The Principal's Role
Leader of Leaders

Key Ideas

- Establishing a school design team
- Leading from the directional system
- Leading up
- Redefining the role of principal
- Using the knowledge development and transmission system

An elementary principal seeks to invite teachers to focus on engagement during the first year of the school's efforts to become an engagement-focused school. As the principal meets with teachers individually, she systematically asks questions such as the following:

- *Can you describe a successful unit of schoolwork that you provided your students?*

- *What proportion of the students were engaged—demonstrated attention and persistence and showed signs of commitment? How did you determine the level of engagement?*

- *To what extent did the students learn what you wanted them to? How did you assess the results?*

- *What about the learning experience made it as engaging or discouraging to engagement as it seemed to be?*

- *If you were to redesign this unit for the same group of students, what would you change? Why?*

If Working on the Work is to become a habit in a school, the principal must exert strong leadership to ensure that this is the case. Otherwise, it is unlikely that the ideas set out in this book will have any impact in more than a few classrooms, and even there, it is likely that the effort will be abandoned after a few initial tries.

Working on the Work is hard work, and it requires strong support and a truly collegial environment if it is to become a habitual pattern in a school. More than that, it requires an environment where the intentions of leaders are trusted and the principal wants to work with teachers rather than work on them. In fact, a principal who chooses to lead such an effort will have to redefine the role of principal to "leader of leaders," in full recognition that teachers should be regarded as leaders and that the type of leadership required to lead leaders is quite different from that required to manage bureaucratic employees, even if these employees are professionals. Thus, given a principal who is committed to the idea that his or her task is to lead rather than manage, direct rather than control, it is important to ask, "What steps might be taken to drive some of the ideas and assumptions underlying the notion of the engagement-focused school into the culture of the school and each classroom in that school?" This chapter suggests some answers to this question.

BUILD OR JOIN A PRINCIPAL SUPPORT NETWORK

Principals need support, just as teachers, parents, superintendents, and children do. Support is especially critical when the principal (or any other person) is doing something that poses risks or produces uncertainty. A principal who is committed to moving in the direction this book is intended to support is probably already involved with a group of other principals who have similar inclinations. If so, he or she should stick with it. If not, the principal should find such a group or create one if necessary.

The participants of such a group should work to ensure that the group's agenda is focused on the right issues: those associated with effective leadership in knowledge work organizations. They should seek to become thought leaders and sources of new insights and suggestions for action. It is especially important to ensure that the group does not degenerate into an "issue of the week" group, where immediate bureaucratic problems overwhelm developmental needs. It will be essential, therefore, to establish and enforce clear norms regarding the nature of the topics to be discussed. Group leaders should take special care to ensure that the group focuses on developing new understanding rather than acting as a problem-solving group. One way to do this is to organize the group around a common set of beliefs and then use these beliefs to discipline discussions and establish priorities for study and reflection. Another way to move such a group from a reactive posture to a more proactive mode is to make reading and discussions about what is read a regular part of the group activity. (Sometimes principals complain that they do not have time to read. In the face of such a complaint I once said, "If you don't have time to read, it is for darn sure you will not have time to lead." I think I was right then, and my experience over the past decade has done nothing to dissuade me of this view.)

GET YOUR OWN BELIEFS CLEAR

Before principals can lead others on the difficult road to increased student engagement, they must be very clear about what they believe about the nature of the enterprise they are trying to lead. If you (and I am speaking to principals here) decide to go down the path suggested in this book, it is imperative that you determine that you can embrace and act on the assumptions associated with the Working on the Work framework. It is not enough for teachers to be skilled in designing engaging work; the schools in which they teach must be supportive of their efforts. This means the schools must be transformed from bureaucratic structures into learning organizations.

This is not an easy or simple task. Indeed, I have spent a great deal of time discussing the nature of this transformation in an earlier book, *Leading for Learning: How to Transform Schools into Learning Organizations*, and I recommend that principals who are committed to moving in the direction suggested here read this book and talk with colleagues about it.

One of the most important initial actions for a principal is to ensure that the directional system is in order and that there is a shared understanding among the faculty and between the faculty and the principal regarding the direction in which the organization is headed. A sensible place to begin this discussion is with the principal's beliefs. Indeed, I argue that the first thing the principal who would lead such an effort must do is to become certain that his or her own beliefs are well articulated, for those beliefs will necessarily affect whatever discussions faculties might have about the direction of the school.

In addition to deciding whether assumptions that undergird the Working on the Work perspective can be embraced, it is important for principals to come to grips with what they believe about other important matters of concern to school leaders. In my book *Inventing Better Schools*, I set out what I believe are the most important questions leaders need to ask themselves regarding schools and schooling. Developing answers to these questions is a highly personalized matter.

The quest for a well-grounded set of beliefs to guide action is a continuous one. I have determined my own beliefs to be as follows:

- Every child can learn more than he or she is now learning in school if the child is provided with schoolwork that he or she finds engaging.

- Engaging schoolwork is just as likely as any other schoolwork to be trivial work unless it requires the student to acquire and use disciplined knowledge and to develop skills, attitudes, and habits of mind that give him or her access to, and a preference for, knowledge that is critically held rather than simply received.

- Equity and excellence are mutually supportive values. They should be applied to every decision made that affects life in public schools.

- The key questions for those who are making decisions that affect schools are these: Is it just? Is it fair? Is it reasonable? Is it theoretically and empirically defensible? Is it right?

- In a democracy, the ends of education have to do with ensuring that each child has attained sufficient mastery of reading, writing, arithmetic, and oral communication and that he or she can easily access the knowledge available in the culture and can communicate to others what he or she knows or wants to know.

- In a democracy, no one can be considered adequately educated who does not possess a basic understanding of the core academic disciplines or have a general understanding of the historic, cultural, and social forces that are shaping his or her life.

- The purpose of school is to ensure that each student is provided with experiences that are engaging to the student and from which the student learns those things outlined in the previous items in this list.

- The ends of education are distinguishable from the purpose of schools. Education is a social institution that contains expressions of values and beliefs. Schools are complex social organizations that operate in the context of the educational institution to produce results that are consistent with and supportive of the institutional values being expressed.

- For schools to serve their purposes, they must be organized around students and the needs students bring with them to school, and they must provide students with work (experiences) that responds to these needs.

- For schools to serve their purposes, they must be transformed into a student-centered, engagement-focused learning organization.

- The key to the survival of public education in America is the development of a cadre of school leaders who have a clear grasp of the purpose of schools: ensuring that every child, every day, is provided with engaging work to do that results in the child's learning something that is important to the child and the continuation of the culture. Leaders also must be skilled in creating the conditions in the systems they lead (schools and school districts) that support the changes needed to enable the schools to serve their purpose.

- Schools and school districts are generally inept at bringing about the kind of transformational changes that are required if the schools are to serve the educational ends they must serve. Furthermore, few educational leaders are prepared to attend to creating the kinds of conditions in their organizations that would make them adept at change. Therefore, leadership development is an essential element in any effort to improve schools. The job of leaders is to tend to their own development as well as the development of others.

These statements of my beliefs are the product of nearly fifty years of experience that have involved working with many men and women who have—or had—well-thought-out views about how the schools of America might be improved. I have learned much from them.

I hope that principals who are considering going down this path give careful consideration to these beliefs, just as a principal should hope that the faculty he or she leads will give attention to the principal's beliefs. Beliefs are, however, personal matters and will have no impact until they are owned by the person who is expected to act on them. Only when a principal achieves clarity about his or her personal beliefs will he or she will be in a legitimate and credible position to lead others in articulating and clarifying their beliefs. More important, a principal who has clear beliefs is in a position to lead the faculty and staff in collaboratively articulating the beliefs that will guide the school and drive a vision for the school's desired future. This work for leaders of leaders all starts with clarifying personal beliefs.

INVOLVE THE SUPERINTENDENT AND RELEVANT CENTRAL OFFICE STAFF

Transformational leaders, whether in the principal's office, the union office, or the superintendent's office, are in short supply. Therefore, while I hope that many of the principals who read this book are doing so because of activity initiated by the superintendent of schools, experience suggests that in many cases this will not be so. Indeed, many principals and many school reformers have come to see the central office and the people "downtown" as more of a distraction than a help, more of a barrier to change than a resource to support it. Furthermore, there is widespread support in the literature of education for the idea that the school is the most important unit in the change process and that the position of principal is the most important one in the educational equation.

It is therefore tempting for innovative principals and thoughtful faculty to seek to insulate themselves and their school from the central office and go it alone. Indeed, I have been told by principals I consider to be outstanding that the best thing the superintendent and the central office can do for them is to leave them alone. Reform initiatives like the charter school movement, decentralization, site-based management, and other efforts to counteract the negative effects of centralized bureaucracies have in fact gained considerable support because of this sentiment.

As those who have invested much in school change are beginning to discover, however, schoolhouses are inherently part of larger educational systems. The communities that affect the operation of an individual school go well beyond the community that that school can directly serve or influence in any direct way. Eventually this fact must be accommodated in any effort to bring about real improvements in schools.

Because this is so, principals who are committed to leading a school to become focused on student engagement may find it important to invite the superintendent and central office to learn with the school faculty. By extending such an invitation, principals may in fact be setting in motion a course of events that will transform the way knowledge is developed and transmitted throughout the school district—a transformation that is needed if schools are to become learning organizations.

John Anderson, former president of New American Schools, a prominent school reform organization, has observed:

A growing body of evidence demonstrates that neither top-down system changes nor bottom-up school changes alone can lead to improvements in student achievement. What is needed is system change specifically targeted to support the improvement of classroom practice. Our experience at New American Schools bears this out and suggests that it is time we stop debating the approach, recognize that both kinds of action are necessary but not sufficient, and commit to work together to systematically apply what we know succeeds for large numbers of children in diverse communities.[1]

Change can be started at the level of the school or school district, but in the long run, it will not matter unless it affects every classroom. Moreover, real change, especially transformational change, cannot be sustained without support from the community at large. Wise principals understand that the community their school serves, unless the school is in a K–12 single-school school district, is not the community at large. Rather, it is a subset of that community. The only unit that has the potential to rally the community at large behind a change, and sustain a commitment once it has been made, is the district-level unit. Furthermore, the only political units that has the potential to exercise sustained influence over the direction of state policy is likely to be the local board of education and the teachers' union. Therefore, principals who are more concerned with legacy than ego will do well to work to ensure central office support, especially the support of the superintendent and work with union leaders as well.

For principals who work in a school district where the agenda set forth here has yet to be embraced by the superintendent or key office staff, I offer the following advice:

- Invite the superintendent and key central office staff to join a study group of principals where relevant books and articles are discussed. Suggest that these persons lead some of the discussions using materials recommended by the study group.

- Invite one or more central office members to participate in (not lead) staff meetings and retreats where relevant reform issues are being addressed.

---

[1]John Anderson, "Getting Better by Design," *Education Week,* June 18, 1997, p. 48.

- Seek opportunities to get grants from local foundations and local businesses to support some of the start-up costs. Involve central office personnel and the superintendent in the quest for this funding.

- Take every opportunity to explain to the superintendent and others why you are doing what you are doing, as well as describe what you are doing or intend to do.

Remember that great leaders not only lead down; they also lead up. Indeed, the real test of leaders is that they are able to gain support from those over whom they have no control—and especially support from those who have the power to stop whatever it is the assumed leader wants to do.

CREATE DESIGN TEAMS

In Chapter Five I suggested the need to create three types of design teams. The first is the work design team, which typically consists of two or more teachers and may incorporate media specialists, technology experts, guidance counselors, and sometimes students. These teams are usually rather narrowly focused, centering attention on designing work around a particular body of content, set of understandings, or group of skills.

Put differently, work design teams center their attention on creating engaging work for students and conducting action research on helping them to understand how to better carry out this task. The primary task of the principal with regard to these teams is to provide them with the support they need—especially time—and the encouragement and training to proceed with as much confidence as is possible.

Properly constituted, work design teams can also become a vital component of the building-level induction system. (Induction has to do with the process by which new members are brought into the organization and socialized to the norms the organization upholds.) For example, a principal might ensure that each beginning teacher is attached to one or more senior teachers who serve as advisors and perhaps even mentors. When these senior teachers participate in work design teams, the neophyte is expected to participate as well. This type of close-up work with senior colleagues is almost certain to have more impact than sitting in a workshop, no matter how well designed the workshop might be.

The second type of design team is the building-level design team. If schools are to be transformed in ways that support teachers who are endeavoring to design engaging work for students and plan activities consistent with the work they design, it is essential that three systems be strengthened: the directional system, the knowledge development and transmission system, and the recruitment and induction system. (For a more complete discussion of these systems and strategies for transforming them, see my book *Leading for Learning.*) Working on beliefs and developing faculty consensus around these beliefs is the first step in strengthening the directional system. Other steps are developing a clear vision, assessing the capacity of the school and the district to pursue this vision, designing systems that conform with the requirements of the vision, and creating strategies for making the designed systems operational.

Principals with whom I have worked who have been most successful in moving their schools forward on the agenda outlined in this book all seem to recognize that the school's knowledge development and transmission system requires a vehicle that may not currently exist. Like most bureaucracies, schools, are much better at maintaining the status quo than at establishing or changing direction. Maintaining direction requires attention to the future. Maintaining the status quo looks to the past. Schools are also much better at implantation of programs than at creating new systems that will support substantial innovations. In sum schools, like most bureaucracies, are much better at solving problems embedded in the past than at recognizing or creating opportunities and shaping the future.

The intent of the school design team is to help develop strategies that maintain direction, provide new ways of developing and importing knowledge, and invent more systematic approaches to the induction of new members into the new system that is being created. The fact is that as a school pursues the changes needed to support a sustained effort to create more engaging work for students, the principal needs a group of colleagues who will think with him or her about the current state of the school and about the new vision for an engagement-focused school. Therefore, the creation of such a group is one of the most important tasks of the principal who wants to be a change leader. It is this type of group that I refer to as a building-level design team.

The building-level design team is not a school improvement team or stakeholder group. Rather, it is a collection of persons whom the principal trusts and believes are especially wise, thoughtful, and creative, as well as especially attuned to the way various groups and constituencies view the world of the school. These team members should be leaders and should have credibility with their colleagues.

Building-level design teams should be thought of as the essential learning community in the school around which other learning communities will eventually come to be organized. The design team is a group that thinks strategically with the principal about the school's future and that learns together to work on the systems that must be transformed to support teachers in their new roles. The design team can, in fact, be a key component in the school's directional system and to its knowledge development and transmission system and should be looked to as a source of leadership in these areas. Finally, a principal who is pursuing the beliefs and working with the assumptions of the Working on the Work framework will have to strengthen his or her own understanding of the building-level design team's role prior to forming one.

Effective building-level design teams function very differently from most other groups in a school. Perhaps most critical is that the members of these teams are developed and invited rather than elected or appointed. Therefore, the principal will need to spend a great deal of time assessing the qualities and characteristics of faculty members. Eventually it will be necessary to make judgments regarding the extent to which individuals clearly possess the qualities needed to make an effective contribution to the design of the systems they will be called on to think about. Among the questions the principal might ask when considering a candidate's potential membership on the design team are the following:

- Are those I am considering trusted by their colleagues and by me?
- Are they persons who can suspend judgment and consider ideas even when they initially find little merit in what is being proposed?
- Are they more prone to ask "what-if" questions rather than to make "yes, but" statements?
- Are they readers? Are they willing to take the time to read?
- Are those I am considering comfortable with divergent thinking, or are they prone to push for closure and limiting options?

From among these potential recruits, the principal must determine the extent to which they are—or can be brought to be—favorably disposed toward the kinds of changes he or she has in mind. For example, when confronted with belief statements like those set forth in the beginning of this chapter, how does the teacher respond? When invited to participate in activities like those set forth in Chapters Two and Three, is there a positive reaction? It is only through conversations, careful observation, and a great amount of listening that the principal or any other leader can make a reasonable judgment regarding those on whom he or she can depend to share an agenda and push a real effort to bring about change.

A building-level design team is not a strategic planning group, a school improvement team, or a problem-solving group. Rather, the team should function as a group of internal consultants who provide advice to those charged with planning and problem solving. The design team should be an organizational unit expressly charged with considering the future of the school. Its members regularly review and reflect on progress and limitations and examine strengths and weaknesses in order to identify and frame opportunities. The primary mission of this team is to contribute to the capacity of the school to focus on the future and maintain direction.

INCREASE AWARENESS

The process of building a consensus around beliefs and leading from a clear directional system requires that the principal be attentive to issues associated with raising awareness and focusing attention. Sometimes followers do not attend to what the leader wants them to attend because the leader gives off mixed messages. Sometimes, for example, the principal says that he or she wants a focus on engaging schoolwork but never visits classrooms, or if he or she does, it is for purposes of rendering some form of evaluative judgment. An old saying is apt here: "Followers know what leaders expect by what the leaders inspect and what they respect." People know what leaders are "inspecting" by the questions they ask, and they know what leaders respect by the answers they celebrate or endorse.

If a principal wants teachers to improve the quality of the work they are providing for students and to be attentive to issues of engagement, then the questions the principal asks in the teachers' lounge, the faculty meeting, and individual conferences and conversations need to be focused on these matters. The activities suggested in Chapter Two would do much to heighten teachers' awareness of the importance of engagement in their classrooms. Similar activities are possible with regard to the qualities of work as well.

For example, using the school standards presented in Chapter Four as a guide, a principal might spend six to twelve weeks seeking data to make it possible to develop an informed judgment regarding the answers to the questions raised under each of the identified attributes. In addition, the principal might encourage volunteer teachers to engage in a similar activity in their own classrooms, perhaps using the judgments of peers as well as responses from students to make decisions regarding their own answers. Such activity, combined with the activity aimed at increasing understanding of the nature of design and design qualities, would almost certainly alert faculty members to the importance the principal attaches to issues related to engagement. Observing the way individual teachers respond to these matters will also provide data regarding who should be recruited to become members of a design team.

INVEST IN TEACHER DEVELOPMENT

As teachers show interest in the direction toward which the principal is pointing, it is essential that this interest be nourished. Providing interested teachers with relevant books, articles, and materials (such as access to tools and resources on the Schlechty Center Web site—www.schlechtycenter.org) and time for conversation and dialogue with other interested teachers and the principal are ways of nurturing this interest. Helping teachers enroll in workshops—national, regional, or districtwide workshops—aimed at creating deeper understandings of the principles underlying the Working on the Work framework is another possibility. Hosting a school blog where teachers raise questions about student engagement, share their insights about the design of work, and support one another collegially is another strategy. Perhaps the most significant action a principal can take is to work with a teacher or group of teachers to help design units of work that consciously use the Working on the Work framework to guide the design work and share in the responsibility of delivering that which is designed.

BE A TEACHER

The idea that the principal is—or should be—first of all a staff developer is certainly not new. Dennis Sparks, executive director of the National Staff Development Council, has been advancing this notion for many years, as have I. Indeed, one of the early slogans I used when establishing the Gheens Academy in Louisville, Kentucky, around 1984 was, "Every teacher a leader, every leader a teacher, and every child a success." This is easy to say but is hard to do. The Gheens Academy was created in the Jefferson County Kentucky schools to serve as a catalytic agent to inspire innovation and develop leaders. I was the founding director. The Academy continues to function in Jefferson County and a number of school districts have used it as a model for the development of their own academy-like structures; for example, the Cincinnati Public Schools and the Memphis City Schools used the Gheens model to inform their own efforts to inspire innovations in their schools.

In addition to the fact that many principals feel they do not have the time to carry out this function, many also feel that they do not have the skills. Part of the problem principals have with becoming involved in staff development is the tendency to confuse staff development with stand-and-deliver workshops or what educators sometimes refer to as in-service. Certainly staff development involves stand-and-deliver workshops and even in-service, but it is more than that. Staff development, properly understood, includes any conscious effort on the part of system leaders to develop the capacity of individuals or groups to carry out the tasks they are assigned and pursue the goals they are expected to pursue. This means that recruitment of new employees, including teachers, is a staff development activity, just as are evaluating performance, providing feedback, conferring with teachers, and team-building activity. Staff development is at the heart of what principals should be doing in their role as leaders of leaders.

Over the years, I have been struck again and again by just how important the physical presence of official leaders is to the success and meaning of formal staff development programs. Principals attach more significance to workshops attended or led by their superintendent than they do to workshops where the superintendent is not present. Teachers too attach more meaning to workshops— especially school-based or school-oriented workshops and seminars—where the principal is present and active.

There are, of course, workshops and developmental activity where this is not true. For example, teachers regularly attend university-based training programs and training programs offered by professional associations to which they attach great importance but about which their principals have little or no understanding or are totally unaware. When attendance at such activities is encouraged, supported, and honored by the principal or the superintendent; when persons who attend such meetings are subsequently used as resources; and when the expectation that what individuals learn at such conferences is to be shared, the meaning and significance of these activities are increased. School leaders' attendance at state and national conferences and meetings is an investment that will have payoff not only for the individuals who attend these conferences but for others in the system as well. Ensuring that this is so is one of the staff development functions of the principal.

When the principal walks down the hall and comments on what he or she sees, staff development is occurring. Such comments help to clarify direction, indicate priorities, and suggest alternatives. The adage that followers know what leaders expect by what the leaders inspect and what they respect is nowhere else so apt as when applied to the role of the leader as staff developer. Sometimes the most important work that the principal conducts in the role of staff developer is helping to establish the agenda for those in the district or the school who carry the official title of staff developer. Principals should know the capacities of the staff (not just individual staff members), which will make it easy to identify developmental needs. For example, if principals are to conduct book studies or encourage teachers to engage in action research groups, it is clear that there will be a need for resources to purchase books and materials as well as to provide substitute teachers from time to time. It is also likely that an outside person with skills in group facilitation might prove useful. The job of the principal here is to ensure that the appropriate central office personnel are positioned and encouraged to respond. (If there is no response from the central office or if the central office is not staffed to respond to such requests, the superintendent has some staff development work to do as well.)

The principal has a vital role in leading and giving credibility to formal training activities. Not all staff development activity can be delegated to staff developers. In fact, staff development is too important to the life of a school to entrust it all to others. It is especially critical that the principal be, and be perceived by others to be, intellectually engaged and reflective about educational matters. It is also critical that formal training programs, workshops, and so on that are conducted for school staff are endorsed through the presence of the principal, even when he or she has no particular role in the activity and is already aware of what will be presented.

FIND TIME

Most principals I have met say that they would like to do more staff development than they now do. However, many also say that they feel so overwhelmed by circumstances beyond their control that they lack the time to give personal attention to the development of staff. Indeed, this perception that principals do not have time leads many to the conclusion that try as they might, principals cannot be instructional leaders. These feelings are exacerbated by state mandates aimed at increasing both site-based responsibility and accountability.

There is no easy answer to such problems. It is a fact that the circumstances surrounding the role of principal sometimes make the demands of the role nearly overwhelming. It is also true that there is no way to invent more time. One more time management seminar is not likely to solve the problem.

What then is a principal to do if he or she decides that teacher development is one of his or her primary obligations? Among the things I would suggest are the following:

1. Join with other principals, and do a detailed study of the way you and they use time. Look back over six weeks, and categorize your work as follows:

   a. Things I do that are clearly associated with improving engagement and learning in my school (for example, conferences with teachers)

   b. Things I do that are indirectly but clearly linked to improving engagement and learning (for example, conferences with parents)

   c. Things I do that have no direct bearing on engagement and learning that are clearly important to the effective and efficient operation of the school or school district (for example, meeting with other principals to conduct studies such as this one)

   d. Things I do for which I can see no direct payoff for either the quality of learning or the effective and efficient operation of the school or the school district (for example, attending meetings where materials that could have been distributed electronically are transmitted orally)

2. Given this list, quit doing the things in item d. If you do them because they are mandated by the central office or by the state, join with your colleagues and approach the superintendent with your observations.

3. Ask your superintendent to enlist the support of the school board and local political leaders to encourage the state to remove onerous paperwork tasks or at least to justify them. If need be, write a paper describing these tasks and show how they take you away from your real work: being an

instructional leader. Ask your colleagues and the superintendent to join you in authorship. Publish your paper as an op-ed piece in the local newspaper.

4. Carefully examine those things under item c and determine if there are things you might consolidate, delegate, or do differently and more efficiently. For example, if you use faculty meetings to convey routine information, put the information in a memo.

5. Enlist the support of the superintendent in reviewing demands that the central office staff places on you. For example, if you feel you are too frequently at the beck and call of central office personnel, it might be possible to consolidate meetings held at the central office so that all occur on one day.

6. Look at each interaction you have with staff and with students as a training, development, and data collection opportunity. When you walk down the hall, record what you see, and later transfer (or have an assistant transfer) what you observe to a data management system. If you do not have a data management system, get one. If you have a computer, you have the capacity to have such a system.

7. Try to get an administrative intern or seek to release, for part of each day, a teacher who aspires to be a principal to assist you with routine tasks, data collection, and data management.

8. Never hold a meeting or a conference with teachers where you do not at some point discuss issues related to engagement and quality work.

9. Work with central office staff developers to ensure that the programs they offer teachers in your school are aligned with your intentions and direction. When they are not, insist on changes. If necessary, enlist the support of the superintendent.

The only way to get more time is to quit doing some things that are now being done, do things differently, or co-opt the time of others to do some of the things you now do. The list of advice for principals on time management is illustrative, not definitive. What it illustrates, however, is that the role of principal cannot be changed until principals learn to enlist the support of those who help define that role. Changing the role of principal requires involving the superintendent, the central office staff, teachers, and eventually parents, boards of education, and state education agencies.

INVENTING THE FUTURE

The role of the principal has changed dramatically in the past few decades. In some cases, these changes are due to external mandates and regulations. In other cases, they are due to the changing needs of student and teacher populations. Some of these changes are putting heavy demands on those who occupy the role—so heavy that it is becoming increasingly difficult to recruit qualified and talented people to the role.[2] Those who are now principals have one of three choices:

- Complain about being overwhelmed, and cope with the situation until retirement.

- Quit now and take a less stressful job.

- Work with others to redefine the role of principal so that the job can be done by ordinary men and women and so that what is done will have optimal positive effects on the lives of children and all who work in and around the school.

It is up to those who are now principals to make the role inviting to those we need to lead schools in the future. Much depends on the success they enjoy in this endeavor. This chapter has been written for men and women who are committed to helping to change the system so that the quality of life of all who live in and around schools is enhanced.

[2]See for example, Steve Farkas and others, *Trying to Stay Ahead of the Game: Superintendents and Principals Talk About School Leadership* (New York: Public Agenda, 2001).

The Superintendent's Role
Moral and Intellectual Leader

> **Key Ideas**
> - Capacity building
> - Relationship with principals
> - Shared authority
> - Strategic thinking and acting
> - Unification of central office

The superintendent prepares questions to use in a discussion with a group of ten principals, about one-third of the principals in the district. She purposely convenes a mix of high school, middle school, and elementary principals in order to increase understanding of the district as a whole. Furthermore, the superintendent chooses three different books to use over the course of the year in these discussion groups in order to illustrate and emphasize ideas that are important for these leaders to explore together. Because she wants to guide principals in thinking of themselves not only as leaders of their buildings but as leaders who are part of the office of the superintendent, the superintendent always uses some variation of the following questions:

- *What specific implications does this book have for elementary, middle, or high schools?*

- *What implications does this book have for our district as a whole?*

- *As district leaders, what ideas in this book warrant further thought or action on behalf of all the children and young people we serve?*

Most of the matters that occupy the attention of a superintendent impose themselves on the superintendent. It is the rare superintendent who finds ways to be proactive in a world that seems to demand reaction. Given the other demands on schedules, it is little wonder that many superintendents, especially in large school systems, give relatively little attention to working directly with principals and with teachers. School finance, school board relationships, legal issues, community relations, and labor relations dominate the agenda for superintendents.

Consequently, those who write books and conduct seminars for superintendents are more likely to attend to these topics than to the subject of superintendent-principal relationships. In addition, because most superintendents have at one time been principals, they often assume that they have a clear notion of how to work with principals. That assumption is likely to be wrong. Being a principal does not prepare one to lead principals any more than once having been a teacher—even a good one—prepares one to lead teachers.

Discussions of the role of the superintendent seldom focus on the relationship between the superintendent and building principals. Yet my experience suggests that the relationship between the superintendent and building principals, more than any other factor, explains the ability of school districts to ensure that building-level change efforts are sustained beyond the tenure of the initiating principal and that whatever positive effects there are become distributed throughout the system. When that relationship is strong and mutually supportive, good things can happen throughout the district, even when the initiating source is a single school building. When the relationship is fragile or antagonistic, whatever changes occur in a single school building will be isolated and temporary.

Unfortunately many school districts are organized in ways that insulate the superintendent from meaningful and routine direct interaction with principals. For example, in large school districts, the superintendent only rarely is involved in the evaluation of the performance of principals. This task is usually delegated to one or more deputy superintendents, area superintendents, or directors. The only time the superintendent becomes involved is when disciplinary action is called for or some high-profile honor is to be bestowed. It is equally unusual, especially in megadistricts, for the superintendent to meet regularly with principals, especially in settings where significant interaction might occur (for example, in groups of fifteen to twenty principals). Even large group meetings where the superintendent is a key figure are frequently rare and mostly ceremonial in nature.

Of course, many superintendents regularly visit schools and engage in dialogue with individual teachers and principals. However, too few of these superintendents routinely communicate to other principals in the district what they are seeing and hearing. Indeed, in large school systems, the fact of these visits is sometimes not known except to the relatively few principals and teachers who directly experience them. Thus, the power of the visit is lost on the system generally, although it may be quite significant in the life of a particular school.

As an example of one way this problem might be addressed, one superintendent of a large school district with whom I have worked visits at least one school each week. Working with a designated assistant, he immediately constructs an e-mail letter to all principals describing his visit and the things he has seen that seem to him to be moving in the right direction. This has the effect of letting all principals know that the superintendent is "in the schools," and it also sends powerful messages regarding what is expected and what is respected. Sam Walton used a similar technique to give consistent direction to his growing business. Few managers at a Walmart store were unaware that Sam Walton might be in their store next week. This gave leadership a clear face and a name.

SHARED AUTHORITY VERSUS DELEGATION

Delegating authority is not the same as sharing it. Delegating authority means to assign someone the right to make decisions regarding specified matters without consultation with superiors, so long as the decisions are made within the context of predetermined rules. Indeed, the primary decisions in a rationalized system—a bureaucracy—that are dependent on delegated authority for command and control are those about which rules to apply. Once a decision is made, the course of action should be clear. If it is not, there is a need for more rules.

Sharing authority means that those who are entitled by their organizational position to exercise authority transmit that authority to others and empower them to exercise this authority on their behalf or in concert with them. However, the authority being exercised continues to have its locus in the office from which it is transmitted, and the occupant of that office is fully accountable for its use. Delegated authority can be assigned; shared authority can only be communicated. Delegated authority can be rationalized and impersonal; shared authority is affective and highly personalized. Shared authority must be felt and believed. By way of analogy, delegated authority operates something like a lease on a house. As long as contractual agreements are maintained, the lessee's right to privacy and personal control is protected. The landlord still owns the property but has temporarily relinquished the right to use it to the lessee.

Shared authority is more like the relationship between the married couple who lives in the house. Each has his or her own identity, but the significance of the union goes beyond legal agreements. Each participates in the public identity of the other, and each gives to the other without the formal expectation of a quid pro quo (usually). The strength of the marriage is found in the tacit understandings and informal agreements that surround it more than in legal agreements. The legal agreements can be severed through divorce, but when a divorce occurs, it is likely that the tacit understandings on which the marriage was based had disappeared long before, or perhaps they never were developed and articulated.

Change requires the exercise of authority. It requires, for example, that resources be assigned or made available, including the time and talent of people, the most precious resource of all. As long as the changes are only procedural or technical, the authority needed can be assigned or delegated. A new office can be created to direct a project, and the project director can be given sufficient budgetary authority to act. However, structural and cultural change, the school transformation required by the Working on the Work framework, requires more than changes in techniques and procedures. It requires as well changes in rules, roles, and relationships and changes in beliefs, values, commitments, and orientations. This requires the exercise of moral authority. Moral authority cannot be delegated, but it can be shared. If schools are to be transformed, the moral authority of the superintendent's office must be available to support the changes that will be needed.

INNOVATIONS THAT REQUIRE SYSTEMIC CHANGE

Social systems are a relatively permanent and predictable set of relationships between and among rules and roles that define behavior within a group. Social systems also include the set of beliefs, values, and shared commitments that give meaning to the rules and roles. When educational leaders speak of systemic reform, the systems to which they usually refer are the operating systems that define the work flow of a school or a school district: finance, human resources, instruction, and so on. When I speak of systemic change, I am referring to social systems that provide the context within which all of these other systems operate—or fail to operate.

Continuous innovation is one of the characteristics of a transformed school district. Some innovations are compatible with the existing social systems and therefore require little in the way of changes in the roles, rules, and relationships between roles and rules in a school or a district. Other innovations are incongruent with the existing social systems—that is, the roles, rules, and relationships between roles and rules in a school or a district—and to be effective, there must be accommodating changes in one or more of the systems that define the way work is done in the organization.

Clayton Christensen refers to the former types of innovations as sustaining innovations and the latter as disruptive innovations.[1] I first recognized this phenomenon in the early 1970s when I was trying to understand why many of the National Science Foundation curriculum materials failed to be sustained in schools. Rather than working the magnificent changes it was hoped they would work, I noted in my book *Teaching and Social Behavior: Toward an Organizational Theory of Instruction* that these materials were either expelled from the system or domesticated in a way that made them compatible with the system, though less potent than they might have been. Based on these observations, I concluded that some curriculum innovations fit existing systems, and some do not. In bureaucracies, innovations that do not fit the system are disruptive and will be expelled or domesticated. More recently I have come to understand that in the more flexible culture of the learning organization, no innovation is inherently disruptive. I wrote in *Leading for Learning: How to Transform Schools into Learning Organizations* that when the innovation is consistent with the direction of the organization and accomplishes what it promises to accomplish, all the other systems are adjusted to accommodate it.

In bureaucratically organized schools and school districts, the Working on the Work framework brings with it disruptive change in a number of ways. Thinking of and treating students as volunteers, customers, and knowledge workers requires a dramatic departure in how we have traditionally thought about and treated students. For example, in bureaucratically organized schools, one common definition of students is "student as product," and the quality of schools is judged by the ability of the school to produce products that meet predetermined standards.

As teachers and principals come to view students differently, they are required to think of their own role in new ways. If students are volunteers and customers, teachers are no longer the "sage on the stage," a deliverer of "scripted curriculum,"

[1]See Clayton M. Christensen, *The Innovator's Dilemma* (Boston: Harvard Business School Press, 1997).

or workers on an assembly line. If students are perceived to be knowledge workers, teachers will be expected to design learning experiences that propel students to seek the knowledge they need to create meaningful products.

Teachers who embrace their role as leader, designer, and guide to instruction will come in direct conflict with other teachers or a principal who views teachers as those who deliver a standardized curriculum—a one-size-fits-all approach. If principals come to view themselves as leaders of leaders, central office directors who want principals to supervise and prescribe rigid courses of action for teachers will be in conflict with principals and perhaps with one another. So in order for the disruptive innovations suggested by the Working on the Work framework to take root initially and then flourish over time, the power and authority system, the boundary system, and the evaluation system of the school and the school district must change in fundamental ways.

Therefore, it is essential that the office of the superintendent be involved in leading the changes needed. Systemic change, as I am describing it, deals with the moral order of the system as well as the technical order. It redefines meanings and values as well as procedures and processes. It is, of course, possible for technical changes to be implemented and procedural changes to be installed, such as a new school calendar, without the active involvement of the superintendent. It is even possible to bring about some short-term structural (changes in roles, rules, and relationships) and cultural (values, beliefs) changes in schools without the involvement of the superintendent, although these changes are unlikely to survive the tenure of the initiating principal if they do not gain the active support and advocacy of the superintendent. The reason that this is so is that without support from authority external to the school, when it comes time for that external authority to act—for example, when resources are needed or the principal is to be replaced—the actions taken by the external authority may not be supportive of the direction that has been set by the local school faculty operating independent of the district.

Bureaucracies are designed to reinforce the status quo; learning organizations are designed to invent the future. Thus, the more powerful the innovation is and the more demands it places on the system, the more likely it is that it will be perceived as disruptive in a bureaucratic structure. It is therefore incumbent on the superintendent to attend to transforming the organization he or she is leading into a learning organization at the same time that teachers and principals are being encouraged to work on the work.

A POINT OF VIEW

The role of the superintendent, whether in a small district or a large one, is a difficult one. The demands are already overwhelming. Therefore, to insist that the superintendent do yet more—especially to initiate other things to do—may seem like madness or ignorance. It has been my observation, however, that superintendents who give priority to finding ways of establishing and maintaining direct and vital links to building principals are much more effective at moving districtwide transformation than are superintendents who rely on traditional patterns of delegation, command, and control. There are two things I know about the office of superintendent:

> First, whatever moral authority resides in, or is bestowed upon, the school system, that authority resides in the office of the superintendent. Second, the superintendent can delegate to others nearly anything he or she wants to delegate (so long as the board consents) except the moral authority that resides in the office of superintendent. In the long run, therefore, who the superintendent is, what the superintendent values, and the style of operation supported by the superintendent will be manifest throughout the school system.[2]

To bring about the kind of changes required by the Working on the Work process, moral authority is required. Moral authority, however, cannot be delegated; it can only be shared. That is why the personal involvement of the superintendent is so critical. It may be that a dynamic principal and committed staff can start the changes needed with nothing more than the tacit consent of the central office. But they cannot sustain the changes over time because the changes will go too deep and eventually challenge the basic assumptions on which the school is based and the relationships between the central office and the school. Moreover, if the intent is to extend these changes beyond a single school or a small cluster of schools, the task is impossible without active support from the office of the superintendent. It requires, for example, that the superintendent endorse and legitimize what is going on in a single building as a harbinger of what he or she intends to have going on in all buildings.

Indeed, one of the reasons that so many model school programs and pilot programs have failed to have widespread impact is that they never really

[2]See Phillip C. Schlechty, *Schools for the 21st Century* (San Francisco: Jossey-Bass, 1991), p. 128.

belonged to the system of which they were a part. They became special projects with advocates in the system, but the moral authority of the office of the superintendent is seldom invested in these ventures. The result has been that these projects seldom go to scale and usually fizzle after the initiating principal and core faculty leave the scene. Change can start at the bottom, but if it is to last, it must be embraced and advocated from the top.

The much-touted reforms in New York City's District 2 (an early effort to bring about districtwide school reform rather than a schoolhouse by schoolhouse approach) would not have advanced as they have if the superintendent had not invested his authority behind these reforms. It is instructive as well that when an effort was made to replicate the experience in District 2 in the San Diego school district, the effort failed precisely because it was mandated top-down without attending to the need to involve principals and teachers in decision making. It is important, therefore, to understand that the argument for active leadership from the office of the superintendent is not one for top-down management of change initiatives. Rather, it is an argument that transformational change requires sharing authority, and the sharing needed requires a mutualism that is hard to find inside the context of bureaucracies.

This means that the superintendent who would lead transformation needs to be willing to risk what the principal is risking. Such sharing of risks requires a great deal more trust and personal involvement than does delegation and the "plausible deniability" that delegation provides. Sharing authority assumes a personalized system and accepts the nonrational elements of emotion and affect and of the undertaking. Great leaders keep their egos behind their work. They give away their own successes to others and absorb the failures of others as their own.

THE WISDOM OF OTHERS

Based on over forty years of my personal experience working with literally hundreds of superintendents and the collective experience of the Schlechty Center staff over more than twenty years, I am convinced that if the kind of change envisioned in the Working on the Work framework is to be real, substantial, and widespread throughout a school district, the superintendent must own—and be perceived as owning—the direction that the change indicates. Furthermore, it is not enough for the superintendent to endorse the change; he or she must be, and must be perceived to be, leading it. What, then, should the superintendent do? How might the superintendent provide the kind of leadership needed and at the same time be sufficiently responsive to the other demands of the role to survive and thrive in what often seems a hostile and unsupportive environment?

In my role as consultant and sometimes advisor to superintendents across the United States and Canada, I have been in a relatively unique position to observe some great leaders work their way through the problems they must address to transform the systems they lead. As a result, I have learned much from studying how change leaders function in school settings as well as in other types of organizations—for example, in businesses, churches, and hospitals. What I have learned from these wise leaders, as well as from some who were not so wise, may be instructive to superintendents who are seeking to work out answers for themselves.

Be Clear About What You Believe

As with principals and other leaders, well-articulated and well-grounded beliefs are the bedrock from which all personal action flows, just as shared beliefs are the foundation of clear direction for the organization being led. It is critical that the superintendent be clear about what he or she assumes and believes about the enterprise being led. If the direction suggested in the preceding chapters is to be pursued, superintendents, as well as principals, need to take the time to examine the assumptions underlying the Working on the Work framework and decide whether they can enthusiastically endorse them. If they cannot, they need to say so. If they can and do, they need to say so. They also need to be clear about how these assumptions square with their personal beliefs about school. This means that they need to articulate their beliefs clearly and let what they believe be known—especially known by the principals on whom they must depend if what they envision is ever to be realized.

Personalize Your Relationship with Principals

Principals are key operatives in any systemic change effort. In a well-operating system, principals are like the Roman god Janus—they look out from the school and in from the central office. It is through the principal that the direction of the district is transmitted to those inside the school. The closer the principal is to the superintendent, the more likely the principal will identify personally with the direction that the superintendent supports. Therefore, the superintendent who wants to influence what goes on in schools must develop personal relationships with all the principals in the district. Without clear and personal communication from and with the superintendent, principals are left to wonder whether those to whom the superintendent has delegated authority are speaking with fidelity and whether the messages they give are the ones the superintendent intends. This is particularly true when that which is being communicated is affective and moral in nature rather than simply technical and procedural.

In operational terms, a superintendent can develop and sustain such a relationship in a number of ways—for example:

- Use e-mail and invite principals to communicate directly with you. Be sure to respond within twenty-four hours to any principal's query or concern. This interaction (if you are not already doing this) will require less than an hour a day, and you can determine when that hour will be.

- Commit to meeting personally with every principal in the district for at least three hours each month in groups of no more than twenty-five.

- Put your beliefs in writing (mine are listed in the previous chapter), and ask the principals to respond to what you believe.

- Make most of the meetings you have with principals developmental, not business, meetings. Take the opportunity to be a teacher of the principals who work in your district. Suggest books for them to read, and then discuss these books in terms of their implications for the direction you are setting. You may want the assistance of someone who is good at designing high-quality staff development activities, but you should be the point person every time. This activity is too important to delegate, even to those to whom you have already delegated the authority to evaluate principals.

- Play a central role in whatever evaluation the principals in your district undergo. In districts with fewer than twenty principals, you should personally be involved in these evaluations. In larger districts, you may need to delegate evaluative authority to others, but then you should be sure to assess these evaluations as part of your appraisal of those to whom authority has been delegated. Remember that people know what you expect by what you inspect and what you respect.

- Visit at least one school each week, and report to all principals, perhaps through e-mail chats, on what you see. Pick up on those things that positively reflect the direction you want to set. If there is something negative to address, deal with that in private.

- Make the induction of new principals part of your personal agenda. Have a conference of new principals in groups of no more than eight at least once each quarter for the first year and at least twice during the second year. Do not be afraid to express your hopes and dreams as well as your concerns.

Except in the largest school districts, these recommended activities should not require more than 25 percent of the time of the superintendent. For the superintendent who is committed to having an impact on the quality of experiences of students in schools, this seems a small investment. If you cannot find the time in your schedule to do these things, maybe it is time that you and your board of education consider ways of redefining your role and the community's expectations of that role so that you do have the time you need.

Clarify the Vision

I described in detail in Chapter Four the kind of school envisioned in the Working on the Work framework. But even with this detail, much more needs to be said to make the vision complete. Sometimes a superintendent may use stories about the future to communicate parts of the vision. Other times, the superintendent may simply elaborate in remarks at a board meeting or a communitywide gathering on a particular part of the vision. Indeed, such visions are never complete; they are always in the process of becoming. For example, nothing in Chapter Four addresses how the central office should relate to individual schools. There is no clear and definitive statement regarding the ends of education: what students should learn and why they should learn these things. These matters too, many of which I address in *Leading for Learning*, deserve serious consideration by principals and by teachers.

Discussions of matters such as these are sometimes started as the result of an accreditation visit by a regional accrediting agency or a strategic planning process. I have found, however, that such discussions are usually superficial; when they are not superficial, they are confined to a limited number of persons and a particular period of time. What are needed are ongoing conversations about these matters. Only the superintendent has the moral authority required to ensure that such difficult discussions go forward in anything beyond a ritual fashion.

Among the things a superintendent might do to promote such discussions are these:

- Meet with principals and discuss the descriptors of an engagement-focused school as set forth in Chapter Four.

- Ask each principal to work with a central office staff member to develop a profile of his or her school that provides a data-based description of the school and is responsive to the questions listed under the twelve descriptors in Chapter Four. Principals might combine this with efforts they are undertaking with the faculty of their schools.

- Encourage building-level design teams to base their thinking about change on assessments associated with the Working on the Work framework.

- Create opportunities for the central office to hear from building-level design teams.

- Develop a district design team that you lead. The team should include not only some central office leaders who are open to learning about systemic change and supportive of the Working on the Work framework but also some principals and teacher leaders who will work with you to focus on the future. Keep in mind that these teams are not strategic planning groups or district improvement teams. They are composed of thoughtfully selected leaders from across the district who commit to think with and consult with the superintendent about the future of the district.

- Require all central office staff to participate in discussions of the Working on the Work framework and an exploration of how they will redefine their roles to become capacity builders.

- Require all central office staff to present action plans regarding ways they can provide support to building principals and teachers as they go about employing the Working on the Work framework.

- Facilitate meetings between principals and the central office in which principals enter into discussion and dialogue with central office leaders about their plans to support schools. If relationships are to change between principals and the central office, superintendents will need to lead such change efforts.

- Encourage those who evaluate principals to structure their evaluation in terms that are consistent with the Working on the Work framework.

- Encourage principals to focus on engagement, the design of learning experiences, and the responses of students in their discussions with teachers and their appraisals of teachers.

Unify Central Staff

To develop sound relationships with principals, superintendents must ensure that those who work in and around the central office, especially those who are perceived by principals to have the superintendent's ear, share a common set of beliefs and a common vision. Furthermore, the superintendent must ensure that the beliefs and vision that central office staff espouse—publicly and in private conversations—are consistent with those of the superintendent. In fact, the superintendent must develop central office leaders who see themselves as extensions of the office of the superintendent.

Because this matter of unifying central office is often not attended to, principals frequently complain of "too much centralization" when the problem is more aptly described as too little centralization at the top. For example, principals frequently complain about spending too much time at the central office in meetings. Each department head, operating independently, calls only one meeting per month, but there may be ten department heads. This occurs because the central office is not centralized rather than because the system is too centralized. More important, the messages given off in these meetings may be inconsistent and contradictory. One department may be pushing schools and principals to adopt a program or activity that another department head openly disparages in staff meetings. The human resource department may be recruiting teachers with an eye toward ensuring the presence of well-educated and creative teachers, whereas the line administrator to whom principals report prefers strong disciplinarians even at the expense of creativity and intellectual skill.

The confusion that such situations create cannot be overstated. Furthermore, it cannot be stated too strongly that any superintendent who wants to have a real impact on what goes on in schools and in classrooms—even in small school districts—must do everything possible to ensure that central office staff are redefining their roles—not only "singing from the same song sheet" but also figuring out what it means to be a capacity builder rather than a supervisor.

I am not advocating that superintendents employ strong-arm tactics or suggesting that what is wanted or needed is a group of sycophants. Rather, I am advocating that the superintendent give high priority to leading central office staff and educating those staff members so that they understand and are personally committed to the direction in which they are being led.

Among the things I have seen successful superintendents do to achieve this end are the following:

- Dedicate at least one staff meeting each month to a discussion of the implications of the expressed beliefs and vision for programs and activities.

- Link these conversations to assigned readings around the topics to be discussed.

- Begin each staff meeting with at least one exemplar of work by central office staff that illustrates the direction intended.

- Create an environment in which persons who disagree do not feel threatened if they express their concerns, and listen carefully to these persons. They may be right.

- Do not hesitate to confront central office leaders who are operating from an independent power base. Although this task must be handled carefully, to fail to address the situation is, in the long run, to fail utterly.

- Assign central office staff to work with principals to help develop a school's strategic thinking about focusing on engagement. However, make it clear that they are working for the principal, not the other way around. Central office staff may find that they must develop new skills and attitudes if they choose to work from a basis of persuasion and influence rather than power and authority.

- Involve relevant principals in evaluation conferences with the central office staff members you evaluate, and invite these same principals to do the same with those they evaluate.

It is important to recognize that efforts intended to move the office of the superintendent closer to the office of the principals (organizationally speaking) can have negative effects if they occur at the wrong time. For example, I saw one superintendent assign central office staff members to work with building-level teams before many of the central office staff had embraced the idea that they were working *for* the principal. The consequence was that many principals saw the assignment as one more effort to interfere in local school matters as well as an effort to offset earlier decentralization moves.

Another example of a strategy that brings principals and superintendents into a more trusting relationship is the act of involving the superintendent in the induction of new principals. Induction is, after all a high-leverage activity. Indeed, in most school districts, the superintendent who becomes central in the principal induction process will have direct contact with well over half the principals in the district within an eight-year period. Yet it is clearly the case that eight years exceeds the tenure of most superintendents.

The fact is, however, that for change to be lasting, there must be continuity of direction. Keeping one person in office long enough for him or her to make a difference is a preferred strategy. Failing that, the creation of a solid district-level design team is another strategy. Indeed, I would argue that any leader who wants the changes he or she is initiating to last should make the creation and development of a team a key element in the design of a transformed system. Responsibility for maintaining direction must be diffused throughout the organization. Direction is too important to place the burden for maintaining it on any one person or any one office.

Strategic Thinking Precedes Strategic Planning

As a general rule, I am much more impressed with strategic thinking than I am with strategic planning. Just as the Working on the Work framework requires teachers to design learning experiences prior to planning in detail how the experiences will unfold, superintendents must lead others in thinking strategically before rushing to a strategic plan.

Once the typical strategic planning effort is over, more often than not, many of those who developed the plan disappear from the scene. It is commonplace, for example, to involve community leaders in the development of strategic plans, yet these community leaders are seldom asked to assume responsibility for implementing what they have planned. Similarly, parents on planning teams are seldom part of the accountability system that should be in place to support the plan.

It is also the case that many who are employed in the district will not be involved in the planning and may be only vaguely aware that such planning is taking place, yet they will be responsible for implementing it. The result is that in too many cases, after great effort, the plan is placed on a shelf and serves more as a point of conversational reference than as a guide for action.

As I argued in *Shaking Up the Schoolhouse*, one of the main reasons strategic plans tend to be ineffectual in schools is that most school districts are change inept organizations. In other words, most do not have the organizational capacity to support and sustain change over time. Until these capacities are developed, no amount of strategic planning will produce the results intended. Indeed, the first strategy in any strategic plan should be to ensure that the system has the capacity to implement the plan once it is developed—a strategy that is too often overlooked. For example, until teachers come to understand that students are volunteers, it is not likely that many teachers will see the necessity of Working on the Work. Developing such understandings among the total teaching force requires considerable investment of effort with little prospect of immediate payoff in terms of improved test scores.

Similarly, many powerful community leaders believe that all that needs to be done to improve schools is to go back to the "good old days." But the good old days were not always that good, and to go back to them would not serve the ends the proponents of this strategy think it would. For example, in 1950 nearly 50 percent of all Americans above the age of twenty-five had never attended high school. They did not drop out because they did not drop in. Today schools with a 50 percent dropout rate are labeled "dropout factories." I find that such data often shock those who would go back to the good old days, but they probably need many such jolts if they are to be at all helpful in the effort to transform schools.

Until community leaders and many who take it on themselves to formulate school reform policy have a deeper understanding of the issues that schools must confront, the strategies they recommend will be informed more by ignorance and passion than by facts and commitments. Thus, educating the community, especially community leaders, about the conditions of education is a necessary antecedent to any meaningful move toward strategic planning. One of the primary roles of the superintendent and the board of education therefore is to educate the community and inform policymakers.

Enhancing Staff Capacity

To reorient staff members as they would need to be reoriented if Working on the Work is to move from words to practice requires tremendous capacity to design and deliver job-embedded and work-related staff development experiences, a capacity most school districts lack. Educating a community regarding the condition of education and helping it come to a common understanding of the issues confronting schools require school leaders to engage in forms of marketing and customer education that most school districts simply are not organized to deliver.

Until key leaders, especially the superintendent, principals, and teacher leaders, are in agreement about the nature of the enterprise they are trying to lead and until they have persuaded those whose support they need that their view of the world makes sense, whatever strategic plan emerges in whatever planning process will be of little value. This is the reason I argue that every leader must be a teacher just as I argue that every teacher must be a leader. Until these and other capacity issues are addressed, strategic planning will serve little purpose other than to symbolize that something is being done, even though nothing is being accomplished.

THE CAPACITY ISSUE

In the most generic sense, the word *capacity* has to do with potentials and limitations. Capacity has to do with what a person, group, or organization is capable of doing if called on to act. It also has to do with the limits beyond which performance should not be expected. To say that a jar has a one-quart capacity is to say that the jar can hold up to one quart of a liquid and no more than that. A two-quart jar can also hold one quart, but it has the capacity to hold two quarts—though not three.

The word *capacity* is meaningless without some referent. The question to ask about capacity is, "Capacity to do what?" The most critical capacities in organizational life are those to innovate on a continuous basis and adjust critical systems in ways that support innovations.

Because they are organized as bureaucracies, the capacity of schools to install dramatic innovations is limited by a lack of nimbleness with regard to systems change. Indeed, the lack of nimbleness makes certain innovations disruptive in the first place. If schools were organized as learning organizations, there would in fact be few innovations that would be disruptive, since innovation would be built into the DNA of the organization.

It is therefore incumbent on leaders to focus attention on transforming their schools into learning organizations, for only through such transformation can schools develop the capacity to support continuous innovation. Without the capacity to innovate on a continuous basis, the ability to improve schools is limited to improvements that can be accomplished with sustaining innovations alone. Thus, capacity building is both the ends and the means of school transformation.

THE CAPACITY AUDIT

Over the past twenty years, I have spent considerable time identifying and describing the characteristics of schools and school systems that are successful in managing innovations and undergoing the types of systemic changes that powerful innovations require. I have identified three general capacities that schools and school systems must have in place if they are to be successful at supporting and sustaining systemic changes and introducing disruptive innovations:[3]

- The capacity to establish and maintain a focus on the future

- The capacity to maintain direction once a clear focus has been established

- The capacity to act strategically—that is, to reallocate existing resources, seize opportunities, and create a new future, rather than continue to be dominated by the need to solve problems that have their origins in the past

As a part of my work at the Schlechty Center, I have led the development of a variety of tools and processes intended to help school leaders assess the extent to which their organizations have the capacity to support transformative efforts. Based on these experiences, I have found the following to be some essential questions that such an audit needs to address:

- Is there a shared understanding, especially among top leaders, principals, and teacher leaders, regarding the need for transformation and a clear understanding of the difference between reform and transformation?

- Do these leaders share a common vision or image of the nature of the schools they want to create and the kind of education they propose to provide? Is this image supported and endorsed by community leaders?

- Are leaders and teachers clearly focused on providing engaging experiences for students? Do they perceive the provision of such work as the highest-priority item on their work agenda?

---

[3]For a more detailed discussion of my views on these matters, see these two books: *Inventing Better Schools* (San Francisco: Jossey-Bass, 1997) and *Shaking Up the Schoolhouse* (San Francisco: Jossey-Bass, 2001).

- Is the power and authority system positioned to be responsive to supporting system changes needed to implement innovations and foster transformation of rules, roles, and relationships, or does bureaucratic practicality overwhelm the need for developmental work?

- Are educators, parents, and community leaders in agreement regarding the standards that should be applied to the performance of students, staff, and schools and the means by which progress toward meeting these standards is to be assessed?

- Have induction systems, recruitment systems, and executive succession strategies been put in place that ensure that the direction, once established, can be maintained over a long enough time to outlast the tenure of any single person, especially of top-level leaders, including the superintendent and members of the board of education?

- Does the system have the resources, personnel, and commitments needed to ensure the kind of training and development needed to support teachers and school leaders in their efforts at transformation? In addition, are members of the school board and other community leaders prepared to support local efforts at transformation through advocacy at the level of the state legislature and state education agency?

- Are systems in place to protect employees from negative consequences when they take reasonable risks to increase student engagement that turn out to be less successful than it was hoped they would be? Do these systems provide means to collect data that translate failures into learning opportunities?

- Is an effort being made to transform roles so that new technologies become learning technologies rather than teaching technologies and that new technologies are constantly being reviewed, tested, and adopted when it is economically and technically possible to do so?

- Is collaborative action a high-priority item as reflected in the creation of learning communities, design teams, and cross-role, multilevel problem-solving groups?

Using questions such as these as a guide, a superintendent and his or her staff, perhaps working through a district-level design team, can get a fairly clear image of the capacity of the district to support transformative efforts. This capacity, more than any other, should be of concern to the superintendent committed to school transformation. Acting on what is learned, the superintendent can cause the school district to develop and sustain the capacities needed to transform all schools into platforms for learning.

A CONCLUDING COMMENT

I was once stuck on a long cab ride with a former executive from General Motors Corporation. I had just been on a visit to Toyota—which at the time seemed to be in great shape, while GM was on shaky ground. In discussing the matter, he asked me if I knew the difference between executives from American automobile companies and executives from Toyota. I did not and said so. He replied, "Well, American executives are concerned primarily with building great careers. The Japanese worry about building great cars."

Even though I thought his comment a bit wrong-headed, I was struck by the fact that this distinction fit what I have observed among many superintendents. Some seem passionately concerned about building great schools and assume that if they do so, they will have great careers. Others seem more concerned with building great careers and seem always to be looking for the next career move, knowing full well that principals and teachers are less likely to follow them in the difficult work of transforming schools if they are not confident their putative leader is going to stick with them.

Trust in leaders is key to school transformation. People will follow strong leaders if they trust them but will resist strong leadership if they do not trust the leader. It is essential that the superintendent and those closest to him or her be trustworthy and perceived as trustworthy. They must keep their egos behind their work instead of in front of it, and they must give away success and absorb failures that they could well blame on others. Courage and integrity cannot be taught, but they certainly can be recognized—and without courage and integrity, superintendents, like other leaders with similar deficits, are but "sounding brass or a tinkling cymbal."

Rethinking Accountability

Key Ideas	
• Accountability *for* versus accountability *to*	• Standards that matter to students, teachers, and parents
• Necessary conditions for change	

In a design team meeting in May concluding the first year of the team's work, the principal and teacher cochair lead a discussion of what evidence the team can cite indicating significant change in three areas of focus:

• *Teacher collaboration around the design of student work*

• *Use of teacher-made measures of student engagement*

• *Focus on beliefs about the role of student, the role of teacher, and the relationship of these roles*

   Some design team members bring in artifacts to serve as documentary evidence. Some mention changes in school policies and procedures reflecting changes in roles. In other cases they mention anecdotes and comments from colleagues and students. To address this category, the team decides to conduct some interviews of teachers and students in order to generate evidence. They set a target date of August to prepare a case for what has been accomplished as a school to present to the faculty and staff as part of the opening-of-school session. The case will also serve as a springboard for next steps. The group decides that they will analyze test data as well, but that these three areas of focus will be front and center for the faculty and staff.

I n 2007 David Weinberger, a well-regarded commentator, coined the term *accountabalism* to describe what he saw happening in American business.[1]

[1]See David Weinberger, "The Folly of Accountabalism," *Harvard Business Review,* Feb. 2007, p. 24.

In this short article, Weinberger makes it clear how an overly rationalized view of what makes people accountable and how performance can be regulated and controlled leads to further bureaucratization and atomization of organizations, which are among the root causes of many performance problems businesses as well as schools confront. According to Weinberger, "Accountabalism is a type of superstitious thinking that allows us to live in a state of denial about just how little control we individuals have over our environment." He goes on to write: "It spread to schools—where it is eating our young—as a result of our recent irrational exuberance about testing, which forces education to become something that can be measured precisely."

I have long been concerned about this matter though until I read Weinberger's article I could not put a name on the source of my fear. Indeed, at the time I wrote the original version of *Working on the Work*, I expressed concern about the impact the accountability movement was threatening to have on the quality of schools and schooling. For example, I observed that as a result of becoming increasingly embedded in government-based accountability systems, even when leaders think they have clarity about the purpose of school and the subsequent practices they hope to pursue, the state systems are implemented in such a way that being accountable *to* some external agency overpowers any good intentions that teachers, principals, and superintendents might have had to hold themselves accountable *for* the important work of increasing engagement and learning.

This was not and is not a plea for relief from accountability. I believe that there is much that schools control that can make it possible for boys and girls to enjoy the kind of exciting, relevant, twenty-first-century education that their teachers, parents and grandparents, and the larger community want for them and that those who teach and manage our schools should be accountable for ensuring that these things happen. What I find objectionable is the tendency to make the state rather than the local community the locus of accountability and the parallel tendency to hold teachers and schools accountable for things over which they have little control. (For a fuller discussion, see my book *Leading for Learning: How to Transform Schools into Learning Organizations*.)

THE ROLE OF STANDARDS

Paralleling the growth of the accountability movement was the development of a movement toward standards-based education. This idea had been around for some time, but in 1983, with the publication of *A Nation at Risk*, the discussion of standards took on new significance.[2] Among other things, the authors of the report argued that the problem that beset America's schools had to do primarily with the fact that the schools had lowered their standards and could no longer compete with schools from other parts of the world.

The idea that standards are important to learning is certainly not lost on teachers, and they worry about standards constantly. Unfortunately, the strategies that the state and federal government are now employing to enforce standards cause teachers to center their attention on the wrong standards. For many teachers, the standard of concern is a test score, and raising standards means nothing more or less than raising the number of students who reach the cutoff score on a test.[3]

The authors of *A Nation at Risk* had a considerably different view of standards. They were more concerned with curriculum standards than the scores of students on a standardized test. They were concerned with the fact that in the effort to serve increasing numbers of students, the schools had watered down what they expected most students to know and be able to do. They also were concerned that the standards for what should be taught, as well as what students actually learned, had eroded.

The Working on the Work framework suggests that not only is it important to be clear about curriculum intentions and curriculum standards but also that for standards to motivate, they must have meaning and perceived value to those to whom they are being applied. Student performance standards in particular must be stated in ways that have meaning to students. If students are to learn what the curriculum standards suggest they should, then students must see personal value in this work. Furthermore, those who are being asked to meet high standards must be provided the opportunity to test themselves against these standards without the threat of negative consequence if they fail initially. Standards should not be perceived as an end point or a goal. Rather, they are markers on a horizon that indicate a direction to be taken rather than a goal to be achieved.

[2]The National Commission on Excellence in Education, *A Nation at Risk: The Imperative for Educational Reform*, United States Department of Education, http://www.ed.gov/pubs/NatAtRisk/index.html.

[3]Diane Ravitch presents a brilliant discussion of this problem in her latest book: *The Death and Life of the Great American School System: How Testing and Choice Are Undermining Education* (New York: Basic Books, 2010).

If standards are to guide action in schools, school faculties must hold themselves accountable for establishing and maintaining agreements regarding what students should know (curriculum standards) and how they will know that the students know these things (performance standards). This means that what students are to learn must have meaning to the students and that the motivation to learn must be built into the work the students are expected to do to learn these things.

Educators who want to transform schools into places where engagement is central must also hold themselves accountable for thinking differently about what educators control. Many creative teachers have happy accidents that are the result of their intuition and instincts but are not the result of a systematic approach to the design of work. With the Working on the Work framework, teachers gain the insight and control to engage more students more of the time. The Working on the Work framework provides a structure to discipline the design and analysis of the work that teachers provide students. When things go well, the framework offers suggestions as to why this is so, and when they do not go so well, the Working on the Work framework can provide useful insights into what might be going wrong.

I also believe that schools are accountable for exposing teachers to new ideas and a language that disciplines their work and for offering regular and numerous opportunities for teachers to use their new learning in their work as leaders, designers, and guides to instruction. The Working on the Work framework provides a language that promotes disciplined discussions among teachers and between teachers and principals. These discussions can lead to the sharing of insights and thus to the overall improvement of the quality of the experiences in a school as well as in individual classrooms.

As I have indicated throughout this book, the Working on the Work framework is little more than common sense. This does not mean that the framework is without a theoretical base or is oblivious to research. However, what Willard Waller wrote many years ago is as true today as when he wrote it: "In the present state of our science, [a writer cannot] hope to get very far in front of common sense, and he is usually fortunate if he does not fall behind it."[4]

In the nearly eighty years since Waller wrote these words, educational research has done much to bolster our understanding of what goes on in schools and

[4]Willard Waller, *The Sociology of Teaching* (Hoboken, N.J.: Wiley, 1967). (Originally published 1932)

classrooms. Unfortunately, much that researchers have found to be so has yet to be translated into routine practice in schools. Is this because teachers are resistant to change or ignorant about the research? Perhaps this is so in some cases. More likely, however, the explanation lies elsewhere. Again, Waller's words are instructive:

> When theory is not based upon existing practice, a great hiatus appears between theory and practice, and the consequence is that the progressiveness of theory does not affect the conservatism of practice. The student teacher learns the most advanced theory of education and goes out from the school with a firm determination to put it into practice. But he finds that this theory gives him little help in dealing with the concrete situation that faces him. After a few attempts to translate theories into educational practice, he gives up and takes his guidance from conventional sources, from the advice of older teachers, the proverbs of the fraternity, and the commandments of the principals. It is this failure of the science of education to deal with the actualities that largely accounts for the slow pace of progress in educational practice.[5]

The Working on the Work framework is intended to make it possible for practitioners to share their wisdom in a disciplined way and thereby learn better from each other, as well as from the research available to them. The framework provides a language of social motives. It proceeds from a simple question: What is it that students care about that could be built into the tasks they are assigned that would make it more likely they will become engaged and invest great effort in the task? The primary job of the teacher is to work out answers to this question every day. The Working on the Work framework provides a structure within which to develop these answers.

However, as powerful as the Working on the Work framework is, the Schlechty Center's more than twenty years of experience makes it clear that the framework is more likely to yield important results when school leaders deliberately put it to work in schools and districts in ways that coincide with the recommendations I have outlined in this book. The effective use of the framework requires leaders who hold themselves accountable for communicating every day the idea that engagement is a central concern and then providing those who would follow

[5]Ibid., pp. 192–193.

them with the tools and support they need to continuously improve their own capacity to design such work.

SOURCES OF RESISTANCE

It is difficult to dispute the proposition that students are likely to exert more energy and attend more carefully to tasks and assignments in which they are engaged than in tasks where their engagement is less profound. It is also difficult to argue with the notion that students who exert more energy and attend more carefully are likely to learn more than their less energized colleagues. It should therefore be relatively easy to persuade those who are concerned about increasing learning in schools that an effort to increase the number of students who are engaged in schoolwork is a worthy pursuit. Unfortunately, this is not always so. There are several reasons for this condition:

- In spite of the rhetoric that insists that every child can learn at high levels, it remains the case that many Americans, including many educators, really do not believe that most students—let alone nearly all of them—are capable of high levels of academic achievement. For many, high levels of academic learning are perceived to be accessible to only a few. Academic learning continues to be viewed by many as an elite enterprise.

- Serious efforts to design schoolwork that is engaging to most students most of the time probably cannot be successful without increasing the opportunities for collegial interaction typical in most schools today. These efforts also require considerably more time than is available to the typical teacher in the typical school. (If schools, especially high schools, were organized so that teachers spent less time instructing students and more time designing work that caused students to seek instruction, some of the time issues would disappear.)

- The way the standards movement has evolved in the United States, many teachers perceive a contradiction between what the Working on the Work framework calls on them to do and what they are expected to do to raise test scores. Some teachers, in fact, frame the issue as a stark choice between improving learning and improving test scores. Given the pressure to improve test scores, sometimes these teachers do not find the Working on the Work framework inspiring.

Each of these conditions must be addressed if the cause of transforming our schools is to move from rhetoric to reality. Therefore, the final pages of this book are dedicated to discussing each in detail.

EVERY CHILD CAN LEARN

The idea that every child can learn at high levels has considerable ideological appeal, especially to educators who are committed to the proposition that excellence and equity are mutually supportive values. However, to say that all children can learn at high levels is not enough. Anyone who makes this statement is obliged to stipulate what is to be learned and to stipulate as well what is meant by "at high levels."

It is clear, for example, that every child will not be able to learn physics at the level at which Albert Einstein understood this subject. Is it, however, reasonable to expect that all, or nearly all, students are capable of understanding the role Einstein played in revolutionizing thinking in the world of physics? At a more basic level, few students will master the art of writing at the level of Ernest Hemingway or Maya Angelou. Is it, however, reasonable to expect that most students can learn to read at a level that will make it possible for them to appreciate the work of authors such as these? Moreover, is it reasonable to expect that most students will be capable of writing persuasively and with clarity? Is it reasonable to expect that nearly all students can learn to add, subtract, multiply, and divide whole numbers and work with fractions and decimals? Is it reasonable to assume that all, or nearly all, students can learn to analyze arguments critically, recognize logical flaws, and themselves develop logical and coherent arguments?

School faculties must be clear about their collective answers to questions such as these, and they must be prepared to announce their conclusions loudly and defend them. If school leaders do not hold themselves accountable for causing such discussions and declarations to happen, there is little possibility that the Working on the Work framework will genuinely guide the school's work. If the conclusion is that only a relatively few students can learn at high levels, they should say so. I recommend, however, that a faculty that arrives at this conclusion be required to place a placard over the schoolhouse door announcing, "Some students will learn here. Maybe your child will be one of them."

If, however, a faculty sincerely believes that all, or nearly all, children can learn at high levels, that faculty must take the time to define what is to be learned and what they mean by "at high levels." They must also be prepared to act when they find that students are not achieving these standards, and they must be prepared to be held accountable for their actions. Included in this accountability is the obligation to try to understand why students fail and, based on this understanding, develop strategies that promise to correct the situation observed. Only when such commitments are present will the phrase "all students can learn at high levels" be transformed from a slogan and a bit of hollow rhetoric into a guide for action in schools. In my view, this was the original intent of the standards movement, but somehow this intent has been lost.

THE ISSUES OF TIME AND COLLEGIALITY

Although the issue of collegiality has gained more attention in the past thirty years than was the case earlier, the situation Waller described in 1932 and Lortie in 1976 has not changed all that much.[6] Teachers continue to work in relative isolation and with only limited support from colleagues. There is no question that a school that is focused on providing all children with engaging experiences every day will require much different patterns of interaction between and among faculty members than is typical in schools today.

Few teachers, acting alone, can meet the demands that the Working on the Work framework imposes. Collegial support and technical support from technology specialists and persons with special expertise in curriculum design and assessment are required, and this support will need to be at a level that is quantitatively and qualitatively different from that which is now provided. For example, teachers will need to be in a position to initiate tasks for central office specialists to carry out on their behalf and expect that they will do so. To say the least, this will be something of a role reversal in many school districts. Such role changes require that principals, central office leaders, and superintendents hold themselves accountable for causing such role changes.

It is, for example, probably unreasonable to expect all teachers to be able to create digital presentations that support the development of concepts they are trying to teach. But it is not unreasonable to expect that a teacher might provide the framework for such presentations and then supervise curriculum special-

---

[6]Willard Waller, *The Sociology of Teaching* (Hoboken, N.J.: Wiley, 1967). (Originally published 1932); Dan Lortie, *School Teacher* (Chicago: University of Chicago Press, 1976).

ists and technology specialists who are doing the technical work on the teacher's behalf. Nor is it unreasonable to assume that the school district could be organized in a way that makes such assistance routinely available to teachers.

Indeed, if the issues of time and collegiality are to be addressed effectively, what is needed is truly radical (in the sense of "to the root") thinking about the way schools are organized and managed. It has always been the case that academic learning is best accomplished in settings where small-group instruction and tutorials are the dominant forms of instruction. Because such instruction has been too expensive to provide en masse, America's commitment to mass education required schools to be organized for large-group instruction. Today the presence of increasingly sophisticated electronic technologies makes it possible to provide all students with a form of instruction that places more emphasis on small-group instruction and tutorials than has been possible in the past. The blending of digital learning experiences with teacher-student and student-student face-to-face learning experiences holds great promise. These same technologies also hold the promise of giving teachers and school administrators more control over their time and how it is used than has ever before been possible. With this control, teachers could have more time to work together, confer with students, and reflect on their practice than is generally thought possible today.

To take advantage of these opportunities, however, the rules, roles, and relationships and the beliefs, values, and commitments in which these are embedded will need to be transformed. Schools will need to become learning platforms rather than platforms for instruction, and students will need to be empowered and encouraged to pull instruction from their expanded environments rather than having the instruction pushed to them on a schedule that accommodates the teachers' need to respond to conflicting demands for their (the teachers') time and attention. This requires proactive work on the part of all school leaders, but most especially it requires the attention and commitment of the superintendent and the board of education.

THE STANDARDS MOVEMENT, THE TESTING MOVEMENT, AND ACCOUNTABILITY

There is no question that the increasing reliance on standardized tests as the primary, if not the only, means of measuring the performance of teachers and schools does discourage teachers from seriously addressing issues related to ensuring that students are engaged in their schoolwork. There is, furthermore, some empirical evidence to support the inference that teachers who encourage superficial coverage of content are more likely to produce quick results than are teachers who insist on expecting students to be involved more profoundly with the content being tested.[7] This does not mean that students who pursue an in-depth understanding of the disciplines they are studying do not do well on tests. Of course, they do. What it does mean is that getting students engaged in ways that produce profound understandings takes time and is more difficult than is the case if one is willing to settle for superficial coverage. Furthermore, it is much easier to conceive of strategies that produce ritual compliance and strategic compliance than it is to conceive of strategies that produce engagement. Finally, it is also simpler for leaders to forgo the important conversations about what standards for learning should be than it is to accept and move on to the more simple-minded notion that test scores are standards.

The unfortunate result is—or can be—that teachers are encouraged to give preference to programs and activities that result in strategic or ritual compliance and overlook or look past efforts to create schoolwork to produce engagement. This tendency is especially likely to be present in schools that serve poor children. It is, after all, in these schools where test scores are most likely to be below the minimum required to avoid punitive action by the state.

The fact that superficial coverage and strategic compliance can produce relatively high performances as measured by tests has certainly not escaped the attention of many teachers in schools serving upper-middle-class children. Teachers in these schools frequently complain that too many of their students are concerned only with their grades and their SAT Reasoning Test scores and are too little concerned with the quality of the work they produce or with what they are learning. An overemphasis on testing and test scores can only exacerbate this condition and may in fact cause teachers to become increasingly reluctant to explore more intellectually satisfying alternatives. Thus, even in schools serving children from more affluent families where test scores are relatively high, the effects of an overemphasis on test scores can be harmful.

[7]See, for example, J. L. Meece, P. C. Blumenfield, and R. H. Hoyle, "Students' Goal Orientation and Cognitive Engagement in Classroom Activities," *Journal of Educational Psychology,* 1988, *80*(4), 514–523.

Policymakers and school leaders who insist on evaluating schools and those who work in them solely on the basis of test scores make the same mistake as those who base their evaluation of corporate performance solely on profit-and-loss statements. Like profit-and-loss statements, test scores are important. But also like profit-and-loss statements, an over-attention to short-term gains can lead to bad decisions and eventually the destruction of the enterprise.

Rosabeth Moss Kanter has observed, "The fact that money can be counted means that financial measures can swamp other measures of performance and value and claim disproportionate time and attention—even when the counting is suspect. Sometimes financial measures are not the right ones for strategic decision making."[8]

Equally important to profit and loss and test scores is the quality of plans for addressing issues that come up when test scores or profit-and-loss statements indicate that there are problems. Growth and continuing improvement and the ability to respond to changing demographics and market conditions are matters that must be taken into account when assessing the performance of organizations and the people in them. Such assessments require much more sophisticated understandings than are sometimes displayed by politicians who insist on accountability by way of bureaucratic measurement.

A TIME TO REASSESS

As I began writing this chapter, a new book by Diane Ravitch, came across my desk. (Ravitch was at one time Assistant Secretary of Education and a proponent of much that is contained in present government reform policy. Today she is a professor at New York University and a critic of much that she once advocated.) Because I have always been an admirer of her work (even though I sometimes disagreed with her), I quickly began to read the book. In this book, she critiques the overreliance on testing, the distrust policymakers have for teachers, the ham-fisted application of ideas drawn from business, and the idea of charters. She concludes her work with the following statement:

> At the present time, public education is in peril. Efforts to reform public education are, ironically, diminishing its quality and endangering its

[8]Rosabeth Moss Kanter, *On the Frontiers of Management* (Boston: Harvard Business School Press, 1997), p. 278.

very survival. We must turn our attention to improving the schools, infusing them with the substance of genuine learning and reviving the conditions that make learning possible.[9]

This clear and powerful statement by a person as thoughtful as Ravitch, who until recently was in the forefront of those who would use tests and market-driven accountability systems as the primary means of improving education in the United States, is already causing considerable distress among some of her former allies.[10] But as she loses allies, she will find new faces who will applaud her courage and seek to join her in reversing the trends that have been set in motion over the past two decades.

Public school educators who are concerned with issues like those addressed in this book and elsewhere are well advised to study Ravitch's book carefully. She sets out arguments for moving forward with an agenda that is more concerned with what students learn than with simply improving test scores.

GOVERNMENT SCHOOLS OR PUBLIC SCHOOLS

Ravitch and I both agree that bureaucracy is a fundamental barrier to quality education. I would also argue that so long as governments are positioned to control the way schools operate and the purposes schools are to serve, schools will always be bureaucracies.

In a democracy, the schools belong to the public and should be under public control and accountable to the public. The government should ensure that this is so, but we should always remember that it is the public to whom the schools should report. The government is an instrument created by the public just as the schools are an instrument created by the public. Both should be accountable to the public they serve, but it is a mistake to make one of these accountable to the other.

This does not mean that local, state, or national governments have no role in the education of the citizenry. Indeed, they do, but their role is not in running schools or even in determining the social and cultural purposes schools should serve. Rather, the government's role should be as follows:

[9]Ravitch, *The Death and Life of the Great American School System,* p. 242.

[10]See, for example, Chester Finn, "Book Alert: The Death and Life of the Great American School System," *Education Next,* Mar. 8, 2010.

1. The function of government should be to encourage the establishment and maintenance of high-quality schooling in every community in the United States. In furtherance of this obligation, governments should enact whatever policies are required to ensure that every community has an equitable access to the resources needed to ensure that no child will suffer from inequitable treatment because of where he or she was born. The Northwest Ordinance of 1787 stated this well: "Religion, morality, and knowledge, being necessary to good government and the happiness of mankind, schools and the means of education shall forever be encouraged."

2. Local, state, and national governments should ensure that each community and each school has adequate financial resources to provide a high-quality school environment for every child. Each school should also have in place mechanisms for ensuring transparency in their operations and the assessment of their performance.

3. New governance structures designed to ensure that schools are accountable to local communities (publics) and at the same time responsive to the needs of students and parents must be created. These structures may not ensure improvement, but the way schools are now governed places severe limitations on the kind of improvement efforts that are possible.

4. Public schools should be accountable to the public just as the various governments—local, state, and national—are accountable to the public. They should be accountable for ensuring that the quality of the education provided to all children is the quality of education the wisest of parents in the community would have for their children. (This is a paraphrase of a statement by John Dewey.)[11]

5. The schools should not be accountable only to parents or to any other faction or group in the community. They should be accountable to the community writ large, and the idea of community should include all citizens who pay taxes to support the schools. This community is obliged to ensure that the schools are responsive to parents and children.

6. The primary role of government is to monitor the operation of schools and make the public aware of how the schools they control are performing

---

[11]John Dewey, *School and Society* (Carbondale: Southern Illinois University Press, 1980). (Originally published in 1899)

relative to agreed-on standards of performance. It is up to the community to create, adopt, or adapt standards and enforce them. Private schools and parochial schools already operate in this manner—or at least they do so in the main. Local publics should surely enjoy the same rights as do more parochially oriented communities.

7. As guardian of the constitutional rights and civil rights of all Americans, the courts should be vigilant in ensuring that the operation of schools does not affront the liberties and rights guaranteed by the Constitution. When communities violate these requirements, they should be called to account for their behavior. This does not mean that the government should run the schools but it does mean that the government, through the courts, should ensure that local and state policies and programs are consistent with the requirements of the federal constitution. For example, in 1954 the U.S. Supreme Court in the *Brown* v. *Board of Education* case declared segregated schools to be unconstitutional. In 1959 President Eisenhower sent federal troops to Little Rock Arkansas, to uphold this ruling. Both of these actions symbolized the right of the government to hold local communities and states accountable for ensuring that constitutional guarantees do not end at the schoolhouse door.

8. Unlike court intervention, legislative mandates regarding the operation of schools or what should be taught and what should be learned in schools should be resisted. Americans have long been suspicious of the tendency toward making schools an instrument of the state and have been rightly proud of the fact that schools were not under control of the government—especially the federal government. Indeed, the first major effort to provide federal aid to local schools, the National Defense Education Act of 1958, contained the following language

> The Congress reaffirms the principle and declares that the States and local communities have and must retain control over and primary responsibility for public education.
>
> Nothing contained in this Act shall be construed to authorize any department, agency, officer, or employee of the United States to exercise any direction, supervision, or control over the curriculum,

program of instruction, administration, or personnel of any educational institution or school system.[12]

9. The American system of public education was designed in a way that made it difficult to use the schools as a tool for the purpose of supporting the rise of a totalitarian state. When the schools become a possession of the state—even in the name of national defense or international competitiveness—the ability of the schools to support and sustain a commitment to democracy is seriously compromised, and the threat that the schools can be used to inculcate values that are alien to democratic thought is increased. Educators and all citizens must be prepared to defend free public education in America. The schools belong to the public and to posterity; they do not belong to any given set of legislators or government officials regardless of their good intentions.

CONCLUSION

Until recent times, intellectual pursuits have largely been the purview of the rich, the well-born, and the most intellectually precocious of the less affluent classes. In the United States, those who made their living by using their minds and the products thereof (scholars, journalists, lawyers, clergy, teachers, and intellectuals generally) were viewed by the masses with a mixture of awe and suspicion. What was of more value, it was held, were men (and sometimes women) with common sense, a good work ethic, and practical skills.

Today there is a demand for men and women who can think, reason, and use their minds well, and the complaint is that the schools are not producing enough of them. Nowadays the expectation is that the young will learn to pursue intellectual matters with discipline and delight. In effect, it is now expected that the schools will provide for nearly every child a form of education that it was once assumed only the elite could benefit from.

Superintendents, principals, and teachers must hold themselves accountable for providing such an elite education for nearly every child. They must face the fact that the government-sponsored systems of accountability they are now

[12]National Defense Education Act (NDEA) (P.L. 85–864). Available from http://wwwedu.oulu.fi/tohtorikoulutus/jarjestettava_opetus/Troehler/NDEA_1958.pdf.

trapped in confuse mediocrity with excellence and test scores with standards. Schools and those who work in them must approach their task very differently from the past. They must set direction rather than follow directives; they must invent the future rather than simply cope with a future that is thrust on them. I hope that this book, along with the other books I have written over the past decade, will prove to be useful tools in what will necessarily be a long and arduous crusade.

APPENDIX: A FRAMEWORK FOR REFLECTION AND DISCUSSION

Disciplined reflection and thoughtful conversations with colleagues are primary means of improving the capacity to design engaging work for students. To facilitate this discussion, I have used the Working on the Work framework to develop a series of statements describing classrooms characterized as highly engaged. I have written these statements in a way that is intended to encourage self-analysis, but they can easily be used to frame observations and commentary by others.

In addition to the ten categories used in the Working on the Work framework, I have added two categories: one having to do with the need to focus on engagement and another associated with assessing student learning. In addition, based on the discussion presented in Chapter Four, I have included a summary statement, which I refer to as school standards, of the condition one might expect to see in an engagement-focused school.

Each of the school standards is a descriptive statement intended to encourage teachers who use them to reflect on the classes they lead and the assumptions they make regarding the nature of their own work and the context in which that work is being done. For example, some of the questions about content and substance are intended to encourage teachers to consider the degree to which there is consensus regarding the expectations of students. It is not intended to suggest that teachers should adjust their beliefs and "get in line with authority." Rather, it is to help teachers gain a clearer appreciation of the context in which their work is being done and help identify the extent to which mixed messages to students may be the source of problems in gaining student engagement.

To facilitate the reflection and discussion these statements are intended to encourage, I have found it useful to encourage teachers to approach these statements in the following manner:

1. They should make a judgment regarding how the statement squares with their own perception of the conditions that generally are obtained in their own classroom.

2. Once they make this judgment, they should assess the quality of the data on which they base this judgment.

Given this approach, there are five possible responses for each question:

1. I am confident this is so and have data to support my view.

2. I am confident this is so but I have few data to support my view.

3. I really am not sure about this matter.

4. I am pretty certain this is not the case, but I have few data.

5. I am confident this is not the case and I have data to support my view.

Such an analysis encourages teachers to seek and then obtain data to inform judgments. It can also serve as the basis for productive discussions among colleagues regarding the quality of the data used as well as for encouraging a disciplined approach to the discussion of some difficult issues that must be addressed in order to increase engagement in schools and in classrooms.

These statements, if they are treated in a disciplined way, require teachers to make a case for and use data to tell the story of their own classroom. The telling of such stories can transform the lore of teachers into guiding principles for teachers who are committed to becoming designers of work for students. Equally important, the disciplined pursuit of discussion of these descriptive statements can lead to much more creative and productive uses of data than are sometimes common in discussions about teaching and teachers.

PATTERNS OF ENGAGEMENT

Standard 1: Nearly all classes are highly engaged. When they are not, teachers make every possible effort to redesign the pattern of activity in the classroom so that more students are so engaged.

Classroom Indicators

1. Engagement is commonplace in my classroom, and rebellion and retreatism are rare.

2. When designing work for students, I think through ways in which I can build in the qualities and characteristics that most appeal to the motives of the students in my class.

3. When the pattern of student engagement differs from that I want or expect, I analyze, systematically and in a disciplined way, the work I provided to students in order to identify what might account for the difficulty.

4. I operate on the assumption that most of the variability in student engagement in my classroom has to do with the design of the work I provide for students.

5. I regularly invite colleagues to give me suggestions regarding ways in which I can make the work I provide students more engaging.

STUDENT ACHIEVEMENT

Standard 2: Parents, teachers, the principal, and the board of education, as well as others who have a stake in the performance of the schools, are satisfied with the level and type of learning that are occurring.

Classroom Indicators

1. Most students in my classes learn what I intend that they learn and meet the standards set for them. I have data to support this contention.

2. Parents are generally satisfied with the level of achievement of their children in my class or classes.

3. When students leave my class, they are well prepared to succeed in the next grade or in other endeavors where what they are assumed to have learned in my class is important to them.

4. Students I have taught believe that what they learned in my class is important to them and helps them to succeed in subsequent pursuits.

5. Most of the students I have taught have favorable memories of their experiences in my class.

CONTENT AND SUBSTANCE

Standard 3: Teachers and administrators have a clear, consistent, and shared understanding of what students are expected to know and be able to do at various grade levels. This understanding is consistent with such official statements of expectations as state and local standards. Teachers and administrators also have a reasonable assessment of student interest in the topics that these expectations and standards suggest.

Classroom Indicators

1. I am very clear about what my students are expected to know and be able to do.

2. What I expect my students to learn is oriented toward clear and powerful curriculum standards that my colleagues, the principals, and other officials in the school district agree to.

3. I have conducted a careful review of tests, both local and state sponsored), to assess student learning, and I consider these to be both useful and adequate.

4. I am satisfied that the material being tested is that which should be taught to students even if there were no testing program.

5. My view of what students need to learn is consistent with the views of my colleagues.

6. My view of what students need to learn is consistent with the views of my principal.

7. My view of what students need to learn is consistent with the expectations supported by the central office and the state.

8. I feel confident of my understanding of the subjects I am expected to teach, and I am up to date with regard to those subjects.

9. I provide students with a wide range of activities that call on them to work with content and processes that others have identified as worth knowing and worth mastering.

ORGANIZATION OF KNOWLEDGE

Standard 4: Teachers and support personnel such as media specialists generally endeavor to ensure that the materials used to present information, propositions, ideas, and concepts to students are organized in ways that are most likely to appeal to the largest possible number of students and to ensure that students have the skills needed to use these materials.

Classroom Indicators

1. I carefully assess student interests and values and take these into account when I design units of work and identify or plan lessons needed to ensure that students know what they need to know to do the work assigned.

2. I am clear about which students find the subjects they are required to study interesting and which do not. I then try to compensate for lack of student interest in the subject by activities, tasks, and assignments that engage the students even though they are not interested in the subject.

3. When student interest in the subject or content is low, I am especially attentive to designing work that amplifies other characteristics that appeal to the interests and values of my students.

4. Curriculum materials are available that support students' working on and with the concepts, facts, skills, understandings, and other forms of knowledge that I expect them to deal with, understand, and master.

5. I try to employ a wide range of media and presentation formats to appeal to students with different learning styles and ways of thinking, and I receive considerable encouragement and technical and material support from colleagues and school administrators in doing so.

6. Students in my class routinely conduct experiments, read primary source materials, and read books and articles that convey powerful ideas in powerful ways.

7. I regularly assess the skills students have with regard to reading and the use of technology.

8. I make a serious effort to cause students to use what they are learning to analyze problems, issues, and matters of concern to them.

9. I try to encourage students to develop an interdisciplinary perspective—to see how what they are learning in a history class, for example, might have relevance for what they are learning in mathematics, language arts, and other subjects.

PRODUCT FOCUS

Standard 5: The tasks students are assigned and the activities they are encouraged to undertake are clearly linked in the minds of the teacher and the students to performances, products, and exhibitions about which the students care and on which students place value.

Classroom Indicators

1. I always try to link what I ask students to do to a product, performance, or exhibition of value to the student.

2. Students usually see a clear connection between what they are doing and what they are expected to produce.

3. I try to personalize products to address different types of student interests even when students are working on the same product or activity.

4. Students in my class place a great deal of personal value on and take pride in their products and performances.

5. When there is no clear product, performance, or exhibition which to focus activity, I consciously try to incorporate other qualities in the work that will provide meaning and coherence to the activities the students are expected to pursue.

CLEAR AND COMPELLING STANDARDS

Standard 6: When projects, performances, or exhibitions are part of the instructional design, students understand the standards by which these will be evaluated. The students are committed to these standards and see the prospect of meeting them if they work diligently at the tasks assigned and are encouraged to undertake.

Classroom Indicators

1. I make the standards by which performances, products, projects, and exhibitions are assessed and evaluated very clear to students.

2. Students in my classes find the standards used to assess their work relevant, meaningful, and important to them as opposed to seeing these standards as personally irrelevant with no meaning other than to describe conditions that must be met to receive a desired grade or other extrinsic reward.

3. I regularly encourage students to assess their own work in terms of the standards set.

4. I often hold assessment conferences with individual students or small groups of students that address the qualities of student products.

5. I use assessment primarily as a tool to promote student success and only secondarily as a means to justify the distribution of rewards and grades.

6. Timeliness is important to me, but I am more interested in the quality of work products than in time schedules.

7. Peer evaluation and public discussions of performances, exhibitions, and products are common in my classroom.

A SAFE ENVIRONMENT

Standard 7: Students and parents feel that the school as well as each classroom is a physically and psychologically safe place. Success is expected and failure is understood as a necessary part of learning, there is mutual respect between and among faculty and students, and the fear of harm or harassment from fellow students and demeaning comments from teachers is negligible.

Classroom Indicators

1. When students interact in my classroom—for example, in peer evaluations—the interactions are respectful, friendly, and supportive.

2. When a student fails to meet standards but is making sincere efforts, I am supportive of this student and encourage him or her to see such failures as a normal part of the learning process.

3. I expect all students to meet standards at some point. When they fail to do so, I work directly with the student to diagnose the cause of the failure and correct the situation.

4. I provide students regular feedback on their performance, not just when I give grades.

5. My students and I have access to the resources needed—people, time, and technology in particular—to provide optimum opportunities for success.

6. When a student fails to meet standards after numerous tries, I am not reluctant to seek advice from colleagues, parents, and the student regarding ways in which I might help the student be more successful.

AFFIRMATION

Standard 8: People who are significant in the lives of the student, including parents, siblings, peers, public audiences, and younger students, are positioned to observe, participate in, and benefit from student performances, as well as the products of those performances. They affirm the significance and importance of the activity to be undertaken.

Classroom Indicators

1. I regularly involve students in creating products that other students will use, read, or otherwise take into account.

2. I always involve parents and guardians in the standard-setting process and encourage them to function as full partners in the evaluation of the student's performance in school and in the classroom.

3. I often display student work for other adults in the school and the community to examine and comment on.

4. I try to design the work students do so that each student feels that what he or she is doing is of value to others as well as to himself or herself.

AFFILIATION

Standard 9: Students are provided opportunities to work with others (peers, parents, other adults, teachers, students from other schools or classrooms) on products, group performances, and exhibitions that they and others judge to be of significance.

Classroom Indicators

1. I try to ensure that in-classroom and out-of-classroom work often involves two or more students working together on a common product.

2. I try to ensure that student tasks are designed in such a way that students need to work cooperatively to complete the work assigned successfully.

3. I often give students work to do that requires the active involvement of parents and other adult members of the community, including senior citizens.

4. Some of the products students create in my class are clearly intended for other students, teachers, community leaders, and others.

5. I make sure that students in my class know enough about group processes to analyze and evaluate the operation of groups of which they are a part.

6. I design tasks for students that require the use of the Internet and other forms of electronic communication to build cooperative networks among students, as well as between students and adult groups.

NOVELTY AND VARIETY

Standard 10: The range of tasks, products, and exhibitions is wide and varied, and the technologies that students are encouraged to employ are varied as well. They move from the simplest and well understood (for example, a pen and a piece of paper) to the most complex (for example, sophisticated computer applications).

Classroom Indicators

1. I provide students a wide range of material and varied modes of presentation.

2. I provide students opportunities to lead others and assistance in carrying out these leadership functions.

3. I encourage students to participate in educational activities and programs sponsored by groups and organizations outside the school—for example, the local zoo, a museum, a symphony, the Discovery Channel, the History Channel, the public library, a local business.

CHOICE

Standard 11: What students are to learn is usually not subject to negotiation. Nevertheless, they have considerable choice and numerous options in what they will do and how they will go about this learning.

Classroom Indicators

1. I encourage students to experiment with different means of gaining access to and presenting information.

2. In my class, students regularly participate in decisions regarding the processes to be employed in assessing their performance and determining the standards by which their performance will be evaluated.

3. My students and I have access to a wide range of technologies, from workbooks and textbooks to original source materials, sophisticated computer programs, presentation technologies, desktop publishing, and others.

4. I feel quite confident in my skills in using computers and other forms of instructional technology.

5. I believe that the experiences I provide students make a difference in the level and type of engagement they will display, and I know how to work to improve the qualities of the experiences I provide to students.

AUTHENTICITY

Standard 12: The tasks students are assigned and the work they are encouraged to undertake have meaning and significance in their lives today and are related to consequences to which they attach importance.

Classroom Indicators

1. In my class, students see a link between the qualities of products, performances, and exhibitions they produce and consequences that they consider to be personally important.

2. Students believe that they can do the work I give them if they invest the effort. Most of the time they are willing to invest the effort required to do the work assigned.

3. I try to design schoolwork in ways that increase student ownership for the quality of the results.

4. I make the consequences of meeting standards and failing to meet standards clear to students, and they view these standards as important to their current circumstances and future prospects.

5. I design and evaluate the work I assign students in such a way that the success of one student does not have a negative impact on the success of another student (for example, I do not grade on the curve).

6. I try to design the work I assign to students in such a way that they have a positive stake in and care about the success of their classmates.

BIBLIOGRAPHY

Anderson, John. "Getting Better by Design." *Education Week*, June 18, 1997, p. 48.

Anderson, L. W., and Krathwohl, D. R. *A Taxonomy for Learning, Teaching, and Assessing: A Revision of Bloom's Taxonomy of Educational Objectives.* White Plains, N.Y.: Longman, 2001.

Bennahum, David S. "Schools Out? A Conversation with Seymour Papert." *MEME* 2.13. http://memex.org/meme2-13.html.

Bloom, Benjamin, and others. *Taxonomy of Educational Objectives: The Classification of Educational Goals.* New York: Longman, 1956.

Burkett, Elinor. *Another Planet: A Year in the Life of a Suburban School.* New York: HarperCollins, 2002.

Childress, Herb. "Seventeen Reasons Why Football Is Better Than High School." *Phi Delta Kappan*, 1998, *79*(8), 616–619.

Christensen, Clayton M. *The Innovator's Dilemma.* Boston: Harvard Business School Press, 1997.

Drucker, Peter F. *The Essential Drucker: The Best of Sixty Years of Peter Drucker's Essential Writings on Management.* New York: HarperCollins, 2001.

DuFour, Richard "Schools as Learning Communities." *Educational Leadership*, 2004, *61*(8), 6–11.

Etzioni, Amitai. *A Comparative Analysis of Complex Organizations.* New York: Free Press, 1961.

Farkas, Steve, and others. *Trying to Stay Ahead of the Game: Superintendents and Principals Talk About School Leadership.* New York: Public Agenda, 2001.

Finn, Chester. "Book Alert: The Death and Life of the Great American School System." *Education Next*, Mar. 8, 2010. educationnext.org.

Howley, Craig B., Howley, Aimee, and Pendarvis, Edwina D. *Anti-Intellectualism and Talent Development in American Schooling.* New York: Teachers College Press, 1995.

Humes, Edward. *School of Dreams: Making the Grade at a Top American High School.* Orlando, Fla.: Harcourt, 2003.

Kanter, Rosabeth Moss. *On the Frontiers of Management*. Boston: Harvard Business School Press, 1997.

Lortie, Dan. *School Teacher*. Chicago: University of Chicago Press, 1976.

Meece, J. L., Blumenfield, P. C., and Hoyle, R. H. "Students' Goal Orientation and Cognitive Engagement in Classroom Activities." *Journal of Educational Psychology*, 1988, *80*(4), 514–523.

Meier, Deborah. *The Power of Their Ideas*. Boston: Beacon Press, 1995.

Merton, Robert K. *Social Theory and Social Structure*. Glencoe, Ill.: Glencoe Press, 1957.

Otterman, Sharon. "Tips for the Admissions Test . . . to Kindergarten." *New York Times*, Nov. 20, 2009.

Perlstein, Linda. *Tested: One American School Struggles to Make the Grade*. New York: Holt, 2007.

Pink, Daniel. *Drive*. New York: Riverhead Books, 2009.

Postman, Neil. *The End of Education: Redefining the Value of Schools*. New York: Knopf, 1996.

Ravitch, Diane. *The Death and Life of the Great American School System: How Testing and Choice Are Undermining Education*. New York: Basic Books, 2010.

Schlechty, Phillip C. *Teaching and Social Behavior: Toward an Organizational Theory of Instruction*. Needham Heights, Mass.: Allyn and Bacon, 1976.

Schlechty, Phillip C. *Schools for the 21st Century*. San Francisco: Jossey-Bass, 1991.

Schlechty, Phillip C. *Inventing Better Schools: An Action Plan for Educational Reform*. San Francisco: Jossey-Bass, 1997.

Schlechty, Phillip C. *Shaking Up the Schoolhouse*. San Francisco: Jossey-Bass, 2001.

Schlechty, Phillip C. *Creating Great Schools: Six Critical Systems at the Heart of Educational Innovation*. San Francisco: Jossey-Bass, 2005.

Schlechty, Phillip C. *Leading for Learning: How to Transform Schools into Learning Organizations*. San Francisco: Jossey-Bass, 2009.

Sizer, Theodore. *Horace's Compromise: The Dilemma of the American High School*. Boston: Houghton Mifflin, 1984.

Tyack, David, and Cuban, Larry. *Tinkering Toward Utopia: A Century of Public School Reform*. Cambridge, Mass.: Harvard University Press, 1995.

Vail, Kathleen. "Nurturing the Life of the Mind." *American School Board Journal*, Jan. 2001, pp. 19–22.

Waller, Willard. *The Sociology of Teaching*. Hoboken, N.J.: Wiley, 1967. (Originally published 1932)

Weinberger, David. "The Folly of Accountabalism." *Harvard Business Review*, Feb. 2007, pp. 24–25.

Zastrow, Claus von. "New Designs for Learning: A Conversation with IDEO Founder David Kelley," *Public School Insights*, Jan. 20, 2010.

INDEX

A

Academic achievement, high levels of, capability of students to attain, 176, 177–178. *See also* Student achievement

Academic learning, types of, 21–22

Academic values, students sharing, issue of, 17, 18, 20, 47, 102

Academic work, 102

Accountabalism, 171, 172

Accountability: for all children learning at high levels, 176, 177–178; conclusion on, 185–186; and the focus on test scores, 176, 179–181; government schools versus public schools and, 182–185; for issues of time and collegiality, 176, 178–179; locus of, 172, 184; overview of issues involving, 171–172; reassessing, 181–182; and the role of standards, 172–176; scenario involving, 171; site-based, increasing, 147; and the sources of resistance to engaging more students, 176–177

Accountability for the work versus accountability to external agencies, 172

Accountability systems, 5, 9, 115, 122–123, 165, 172, 182, 185–186

Accreditation visits, 161

Action guide, beliefs serving as an, for principals, 136–137

Action research, conducting, 140, 146

Active involvement: defining engagement as, issue of, 119; instruction requiring passivity more than, 100

Activity versus work, 101

Ad hoc teams, 104

Administrative interns, use of, 148

Adverse consequences. *see* Punishment/adverse consequences

Affiliation: classroom indicators of the standard for, 194–195; consideration of, in designing work, 79, 90–91; defining, as a standard for the engagement-focused school, 61; and motivation, 54, 80, 85, 90; questions focused on, for framing conversations, 70

Affirmation: classroom indicators of the standard for, 194; consideration of, in designing work, 91–92, 107; defining, as a standard for the engagement-focused school, 60; enhancing, with discovery learning, 122; and motivation, 55, 82, 85, 108; questions focused on, for framing conversations, 69–70

Affluent students, schools with, 180

Age-appropriate computer applications, identifying, 113

Algorithmic task, 48–49

Alienation, 16, 18, 35

Alienative involvement, 16*n*2, 19*n*4

Alternative view of teaching and an alternative view of students, 102–103; design process reflecting an, 106–108; design teams that reflect an, 103–105; and the means of doing the job, 99–101; and the nature of the work, 101–102; and an overview of issues, 97–99; and professional learning communities, 105–106; scenario involving, 97; and the teacher's dilemma, 99; that provides insights instead of imitations, 108–109

Amish, the, 7

Analyzing, defined, 22

Anderson, John, 138–139

Anderson, L. W., 22*n*6

Angelou, Maya, 177

Another Planet (Burkett), 19

Anti-intellectualism, 18

Christensen, Clayton M., 155, 155n1
Cincinnati Public Schools, 145
Civil rights, 53, 184
Classroom culture, working on the, 86
Classroom environment, 49
Classroom indicators, 188–196
Classroom measures, 72
Classroom profiles, developing, to determine engagement. *see* Engagement profiles, developing
Classroom resource materials, prospective, evaluating, 123–124
Classroom structure, and the tradition of lecturing, 99
Classroom walkthroughs, 27
Clear and compelling standards: classroom indicators of the standard for, 192–193; consideration of, in designing work, 79, 86–87; defining, as a standard for the engagement-focused school, 60; and the design process, 106; and motivation, 53, 86; and partial use of the WOW framework, 122; questions focused on, for framing conversations, 68–69
Coercion, 8, 18, 39n9, 57, 124
Cognitive domain categories, 22–23
Collaboration, 54, 90
Collective assessment of engagement, 28, 28n
Collegial discussion/conversations: about the direction of the school, 135; about transforming schools into learning organizations, 135; described, 64–65; disciplined approach to, 62, 63, 123, 124, 188; framework for, about school standards and classroom engagement, 187; framing, 64–70; need for, 64; over beliefs, 59; teacher's role in, 118
Collegiality, time and, issues of, 176, 178–179
Commitment: assessing, 27, 28; assumption about, 31; conditional, 17; defining, in engagement, 14, 15; effective leaders seeking, 125; and effort, 25; and having a sense of purpose, 122n7; importance of, 8, 20; as an indicator of responses to work, 35, 36; unconditional, 23
Common language, having a, 49–50
Common purpose, having a, 49–50
Common sense, 116n2, 174
Communities: and changing the way they define schools, 127; and the development and enforcement of curriculum standards, 6; educating, need for, 166; ensuring schools are accountable to, 183; expectations of, about the superintendent's role, redefining, 161; involving, in strategic planning, 165; and the locus of accountability, 172, 184; schools transformed from institutions of, 115; support needed from, 139
Communities of learning, organization of, 141. *See also* Professional learning communities (PLCs)

Comparative Analysis of Complex Organizations, A (Etzioni), 16n2
Compliance: becoming the end in view, consequences of, 46–47; black males and, 88–89; defining, 16; drivers of, 45; quality learning requiring more than, 8; reasons for, 43–44; reasons teachers settle for, 125; scenario involving, 13–14; seen as an efficient tool, 38; and superficial learning, 22; time spent on strategies to produce, issue with the, 37; as too often the goal, 103; without engagement, 17–18, 24. *See also* Ritual compliance; Strategic compliance
Computer applications, age-appropriate, identifying, 113
Computer/video games, 43, 55, 85, 85n4, 132
Conflict, direct, with principals or other teachers, 156
Constitutional rights, guardian of, 184
Constructivist approach, 37
Contemporary societies, erosion of traditions in, 7
Content: choice of, importance, 85, 85n4; difficult-to-teach and hard-to-learn, work design teams for, 104n6; emotional appeal of the, importance of, 85n4
Content and substance: attending to, importance of, 81; classroom indicators of the standard for, 190; consideration of, in designing work, 83–84; defining, as a standard for the engagement-focused school, 60; and the design process, 106; and motivation, 52, 84; questions focused on, for framing conversations, 66–67
Context: and culture, motives and, 79; of curriculum standards, designing done within the, 76; for instruction, 50; qualities of, distinction between qualities of choice and, issue of, 81–82; of schools, operating in the, issue of, 8–10; in which families exist, changes in, 128–129
Continuity of direction, importance of, 165
Continuous innovation, 154–155
Control: and autonomy, 45, 92; educators feeling out of, 114; establishing, that does not constrain, 62; increasing, role of choice in, 92; maintaining, weapons for, 9; over effort and attention, 8, 14, 35; over engagement, limited view of, held by teachers, 17, 18; over information, change in the, 7; over learning outcomes, issue of, 56; over time, having more, 179; social, one means of, 26
Conversations: disciplined approach to, 61–64; ongoing, about the vision, promoting, 161–162; results of, finding time to discuss, 73–74; starting, various ways of, 71–73. *See also* Collegial discussion/conversations; Internal dialogue; Student-teacher conversations
Cosby, Bill, 21

Fife School District, Washington State, 104*n*6

Fifth Discipline: The Art and Practice of the Learning Organization, The (Senge), 97*n*1

Financial measures, issue with, 181

Financial resources, adequate, ensuring, 183

Financial support, 114

Finn, Chester, 182*n*10

Focus on the future, capacity to establish and maintain a, 168

Folly of Accountabalism, The (Weinberger), 171*n*1

4-H Club, 91–92

Funding opportunities, seeking, 140

Future Farmers of America, 91–92

G

Game-based learning, exploring, 118

Gatekeepers, 122

General Motors Corporation, 170

Gheens Academy, Louisville, Kentucky, 144–145

Girl Scouts, 91–92

Good students, limited definition of, 17, 47, 102

Good teaching, defined, under bureaucracies, issue with, 38

Google, 10, 108

Government agencies, schools transformed into, 115

Government policy, 127, 139, 181

Government schools, public schools versus, 182–185

Government-based accountability systems, 172, 185–186

Government's role, 182–184

"Grade grubber" label, 18

Grade inflation, 34

Grade-level performance standards, 98

Grades: in the pathological classroom, 33–34; viewed as motivators, 44; working only for, 13–14, 17, 18, 19, 180. *See also* Extrinsic rewards

Grading, and protection of students from adverse consequences, 89

Grading practices, conventional, 87

Grants, opportunities for, seeking, 140

Great Mutation, 6–7

"Great Mutation, The" (Bridenbaugh), 7*n*1

Group work, described, 54

Guides to instruction, teachers as, 10, 58, 115, 126, 156

H

Hemingway, Ernest, 177

Heroic teachers, 49, 117

Heuristic device, 79, 95, 106, 108, 121, 122

Heuristic task, 48, 49

High academic achievement, capability of students for, 176, 177–178

Highly-engaged classrooms: profile of, 32; standards and indicators of, 188–196

High-performing schools, competition in, 89

High-stakes testing, 86

Historical change, rapid, 6–7

Homeschool networks, 92

Homeschooling, 130

Homework, 128–129, 129–130

Horace's Compromise: The Dilemma of the American High School (Sizer), 125*n*10

Howley, Aimee, 118*n*3

Howley, Craig B., 118*n*3

Hoyle, R. H., 180*n*7

Human needs, 45

Human resource department, 163

Humes, Edward, 19, 123*n*8

Humor, 26

I

"Ideal" students, limited definition of, 17, 47, 102

Imitation models, seeking, problem with, 108–109

Incentives: for student performance, 44; for teacher performance, 49. *See also* Extrinsic rewards

Indicators: of engagement, 34–36; and standards of highly-engaged classrooms, 188–196

Individualized instruction, 99

Induction system, 140, 141, 161, 165

Information, access to, change in the control of, 7

Information technology: impact of, on the role of teachers, 10, 101; using, for instruction, 50–51, 99, 100

Innovation, continuous, systemic change required for, 154–156, 167, 168

Innovator's Dilemma, The (Christensen), 155*n*1

Inquiry approach, 37

In-service training, 145

Insight, power of, 31

Institutionalized cheating, 20

Instruction: context for, motives providing the, 50; individualized and personalized, 99; mass, 99, 179; teacher-driven versus technology-driven, 100; and the teacher's dilemma, 99; traditional focus on, 98; via electronic means, 50–51. *See also* Guides to instruction, teachers as

Instructional plans. *see* Lesson Plans

Instructors, teachers as, 10, 97–98

Integrity, 170

Intellectual work, other forms of, 47, 48, 102, 103

Intellectuals, demand for, 185

Internal dialogue: described, 64; framing, 64–70. *See also* Reflection

Internet, the, impact of, 7

Intrinsic motivation: and affiliation, 85, 90; and affirmation, 85, 91; and choice, 92; and clear and compelling standards, 87, 106; defined, 44; and extrinsic motivation, distinction between,

44–48, 80; key to the design of work that provides, 95; and the language of design teams, 105; and organization of knowledge, 85; and product focus, 82; for the task of teaching, 49

Intrinsic rewards: and novelty and variety, 93; providing, 45, 79

Intuition, use of, 121, 174

Inventing Better Schools: An Action Plan for Educational Reform (Schlechty), 57, 136, 168*n*3

Involvement: active, instruction requiring passivity more than, 100; defining, 16; and engagement, 15–17, 18, 119; transforming, 20; types of, 16*n*2

Isolation, 90, 178

J

Jefferson County Kentucky Schools, 144–145

K

Kanter, Rosabeth Moss, 61–62, 181, 181*n*8

Kelley, David, 49*n*3

Kindergarten admissions tests, 39*n*8

Knowledge development and transmission system, 138, 141, 142

Knowledge, disciplined, world of, 53. *See also* Organization of knowledge

Knowledge distribution systems versus knowledge work systems, 9–10

Knowledge work, defined, and other forms of, 102

Knowledge workers, students as, 58, 102–103, 155, 156

Krathwohl, D. R., 22*n*6

L

Language: common, having a, 49–50; of design teams, 105; of design, thinking in terms of the, importance of, 78; of designers versus planners, 50; for designing engaging work, 51–56; of professional learning communities, 105

Leaders: accountability of, 175–176; development of, 137; and how they handle their egos, 158, 170; intellectual, 118; leader of, principals as, 134, 145; as teachers, 144, 167; teachers as, 4, 10, 101, 115, 125–126, 144, 156, 167. *See also* Principal's role; Superintendent's role; Teacher's role

Leading for Learning: How to Transform Schools into Learning Organizations (Schlechty), 9, 38, 39*n*9, 78, 102, 115, 135, 141, 155, 161, 172

Leading up, 140

Learning: academic, types of, 21–22; artificial way of, 100; capacity of children for, beliefs about, 136, 176, 177–178; considering test scores more important than, issue of, 120; electronic, impact of, on the role of teachers, 10; and engagement, relationship between, 117; expectations for engagement and, being clear about, 120; game-based, exploring, 118; for learning's sake, issue with, 20; as a motivator, mistake of thinking of, 78; new ways of, learning, 53; research on engagement and, issue of the, 36–39; single trial, valuing, 54; and trust, 25. *See also* Profound learning; Student learning; Superficial learning

Learning communities, organization of, 141

Learning goals, concern with, 78

Learning intentions, described, 106

Learning organizations: flexible culture of, 155, 167; transforming schools into, 57, 78, 115, 135, 137, 156, 167

Learning outcomes, factors affecting, 56, 58

Learning platforms versus teaching platforms, 9–10, 101, 115, 179

Learning styles, consideration of, 53, 85

Learning task responses, 15, *16. See also* Engagement; Rebellion; Retreatism; Ritual compliance; Strategic compliance

Learning technologies, 99–101

Lecturing, tradition of, 99

Lesson plans, 50, 63, 123. *See also* Planning lessons versus designing work

Lortie, Dan, 83–84, 84*n*2, 178, 178*n*6

M

Market-driven accountability systems, 182

Mass education system, 99–100, 179

Mass instruction, 98, 99

Mass media, impact of, 7

Mass testing, issue with, 39, 39*n*9

Mastery: described, 45; drive for, 88, 91; as a key element in designing engaging work, 45; as a motivator, 45, 46, 53; of other forms of intellectual work, 47; standards that promote, 89; valuing, lack of, 54

Meaning: altering, 78; and assessing engagement, 27; attached to workshops, 145; defining, in engagement, 14; importance of, 8, 20, 81, 174; as an indicator of responses to work, 35; lack of, response to a, 16; learning resulting from tasks that have, research on, 36, 37; and motivation, 53, 56, 80, 93; paying scant attention to, 119; resulting from sharing academic values, 18; standards having, importance of, 173; trust in a, 25. *See also* Authenticity

Mediocrity, confusing, with excellence, 186

Meece, J. L., 180*n*7

Meier, Deborah, 118, 118*n*4

Memorization, 23, 24, 25

Memory, superficial versus profound, 23

Memphis City Schools, 145

Mental models, 59, 78, 97–98

of, 140, 161; influence of, 88; intellectual life of, importance of the, 117–118; language used to describe, 50; leaders as, 144, 167; praise from, 55, 56; pressures put on, 9; primary task of, 81; principals as, 144–146; quotes from, about the WOW framework, 116, 116*n*2; and the reasons they seek compliance, 17; requesting critiques from colleagues and principals, 72–73; supporting, 135; that are engaging, defining, 116–117; trust in, 114; viewed as employees, 115

Teacher's dilemma, 99

Teacher's role: in assessing engagement, 27–28; to become more self-critical, 62; beliefs about, 58; changing the, contingent upon changing the principal's role, 127; as designer, 3, 8, 10, 58, 76, 102, 115, 121–124, 156; to engage students and other teachers in conversations, 64; as ethical guides, 118, 126; to focus on engagement and designing schoolwork, 119–121; as guide to instruction, 10, 58, 102, 115, 126, 156; as instructor, issues with, 10, 97–98; to know and teach the right stuff, 117–119; as leader, 4, 10, 101, 115, 125–126, 144, 156, 167; as more than either coach or facilitator, 125; overview of issues impacting the, 114–116; as performer, idea of, effect of the, 3; scenario involving, 113–114; structure of the, 102; as a supporter of parents and families, 130–132; in systemic change, 126–127; teachers rethinking the, 155–156; traditional view of the, 7; transforming, as requisite, 78, 101

Teacher-student relationship: establishing a, that is trusting and supportive, 89; impact of attention to designing engaging work on, 38; as something that impacts student performance, 4; traditional view of, 7; and trust, 25, 27

Teaching: alternative view of, aspects of, 97–109; art and science of, 21; as a heuristic task, 49; team, 98; type of people attracted to, 83–84

Teaching and Social Behavior: Toward an Organizational Theory of Instruction (Schlechty), 155

Teaching platforms versus learning platforms, 9–10, 101, 115, 179

Teaching to the test, focusing on, 114, 119. *See also* Standardized tests; Test scores

Team teaching, 98

Technical order, 156

Technical support, 178

Technology, defining, 99. *See also* Information technology; Learning technologies

Test preparation exercises/programs, 37, 39*n*8

Test scores: assumption about, 4; confusing standards with, 180, 186; focusing on, 24, 30–31, 37, 38, 119, 173, 176, 179–181; payoff in terms of, immediate,

issue of, 166; and protection of students from adverse consequences, 89

Test-based accountability systems, 5, 9, 122–123, 181

Test-based standards, 98

Tested: One American School Struggles to Make the Grade (Perlstein), 114*n*1, 120*n*6

Testing: high-stakes, 86; irrational exuberance about, 172; overreliance on, 181. *See also* Standardized tests

Testing prototypes, 77

Testing systems, common, 37

Test-taking skills: implication of teaching, and effect of, 119–120; learning, valuing, instead of profound learning, 39*n*8; valuing the learning of, instead of profound learning, 39

Texting, 35

Thought leaders, 134

Threat of punishment, 15, 24, 31, 44, 80; awareness of, in assessing engagement, 27; compliance produced by, seen as an efficient tool, 38; lack of trust resulting in use of, 25; learning resulting from, research on, 36; reliance on, issue with, 44

Time: collegiality and issues of, 176, 178–179; finding, to discuss results of conversations, 73–74; for reading, principals having, 135; required for personalizing the superintendent-principal relationship, 161; spent on strategies to produce compliance, issue with the, 37; that is spent preparing for standardized tests, 38–39

Time management advice, for principals, 147–148

Tinkering Toward Utopia (Tyack and Cuban), 126*n*11

"Tips for the Admissions Test . . . to Kindergarten" (Otterman), 39*n*8

Total quality management (TQM), 62

Toyota, 170

Traditional authority, 43–44, 124

Traditional work, 18

Tradition-based societies, 7

Transform versus reform, 77

Transformation, meaning of, 78

Transforming device, prototyping as a, 77–78

Trust: in assessing engagement, 27; engagement and, 25, 59; and financial support of schools, 114; in leaders, 170; risk sharing requiring, 158; and the superintendent-principal relationship, 165; and the teacher-student relationship, 89

Trying to Stay Ahead of the Game: Superintendents and Principals Talk About School Leadership (Farkas and others), 149*n*2

Tyack, David, 126–127, 126*n*11

U

Undersecretary of Education, 181

Understanding, defined, 22

THE SLEEPWALKERS

VIVIANE SCHWARZ

CANDLEWICK PRESS

First U.S. edition 2013

Library of Congress Catalog Card Number 2012947253
ISBN 978-0-7636-6230-1

13 14 15 16 17 18 SCP 10 9 8 7 6 5 4 3 2 1

Printed in Humen, Dongguan, China

This book was typeset in TWBVSchwarz.
The illustrations were done in pencil and digitally colored.

Candlewick Press, 99 Dover Street, Somerville, Massachusetts 02144

visit us at www.candlewick.com

DO YOU HAVE A BAD DREAM
THAT WILL NOT GO AWAY?

ARE YOU AFRAID TO SLEEP AT NIGHT?

CALL THE SLEEPWALKERS!

WRITE US A LETTER,
PUT IT UNDER YOUR PILLOW...

AND WE WILL COME AND SAVE YOU!

HAVE A GOOD NIGHT!

To You

~~Somewhere~~
~~Long ago~~
Before the Morning
There is a Safe House for You
to Shelter in.

When you are afraid
To fall asleep
When all your dreams
Are Nightmares
Write us a letter
Put it under your pillow
We will rescue you.

Friend

FRIEND frien

It's that dream again.

Everything is made of cheese.

Hello?

I'm all alone... and it's that dream.... But I asked for help....

SQUEE SQUEE SQUEE

FONDUE RIVER

CAMEADERO

SQUEE SQUEE SQUEE SQUEE SQUEE

No! Not again!

7

8

9

Hey! Wake up! I got it!

Oh... very good...

What? What?

This is the one. Excellent material. Good man, Buddy. This blanket has great spirit.

That looks quite powerful!

It smells nice, too. Like popcorn.

We should raise the hero as soon as possible.

Before breakfast?

Do we have time before the nightmare manifests?

Yes.

I'll put the kettle on.

17

Most dreams are good, mind you, or else how would anyone get anywhere in life? But some become nightmares, and dreamers can get stuck in them.

Then we help.

What is a nightmare?

You'll see...

Dream pressure is up! The nightmare has begun!

...right now!

What?

Watch and learn!

Hmm...

WHIRRR

It's a perpetual inertia situation. Standard bottomless, I'd say.

Ah! I have located the dreamer. Follow me!

Come on! Hop!

SSHING

Whoa!

AAAAAAAAAH!

This way.

You're doing well.

Approaching target.

Hey, Buddy! This is Bonifacius.

Woof! Woof! Woof!

Five...four...

Hi, Bonno! Pleased to meet you.

Help!

...three...two...

...one...

Target!

SNAP

21

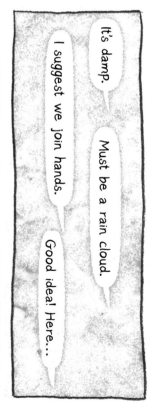

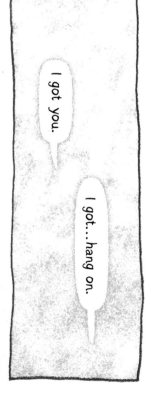

22

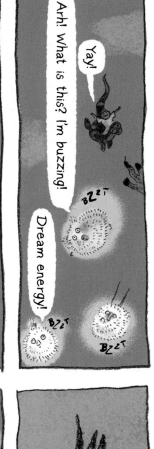

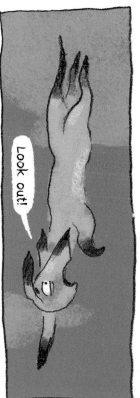

SQUEE

TWEET

I'm going to investigate.

AAAAAH!

KWAA

TWEET

SQUAWK

TWOO

BOINK

BUMPH

Now...how does this work?

TAP
TAP
TAP

Up! Up!

Yes, yes...

Going right up to drop you off!

Right! GO! GO! GO!

How did it go?

He did very well.

Congratulations on your first mission. Rest up now. We'll see you tomorrow.

Uh... thanks.

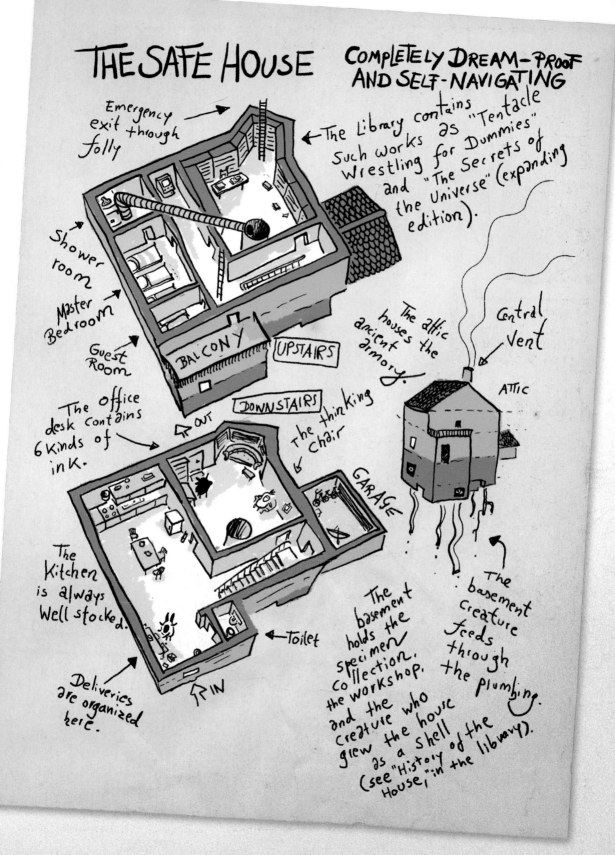

Good morning. I hope you are rested?

Don't talk to him before he's had some tea. It's cruel.

It seems a little boy is lost in a forest.

A forest? Wonderful! Any wildlife?

Very much so.

Oh, my! We must take samples.

SLURP

RRRUMBLE

The house has landed! A new nightmare is afoot.

What? Another one? Already?

Well...not quite yet. Dream pressure is still low.

Let's raise another apprentice, then!

You can be best friends.

Good plan. Where's Buddy?

Wff!

Aaaaaaah. Good man, Buddy. These are just right.

RRRR

Watch this. It's a really good trick. Best thing to do with socks....

Like this... and so...

SLICE

Careful, there!

I know what I'm doing.

I know you know what you're doing.

And some stuffing...

SHAVE

It looks flabby. Let's shave off some more....

It's fine.

Is that how they made me?

Pretty much.

I am stuffed with your wool?

Hardly. Then I'd be bald.

33

There!

Oooh!

Ooooh!

Excuse us for a while.

He looks nice.

I think she's a girl.

BAA: BUMP: BAA: BUMP

BAA:

They're doing the dance!

THUNK

BAA:

Come alive!

Oh, it's done!

SHUFFLE

Oh, oh, oh, there'll be adventure and a new friend and I wonder where we'll go today, oh, don't you?

Well...I hope you like trees.

34

OH, WOW!

I LOVE TREES!

Wonderful! Let's go explore!

YAY! GREAT!

Apparently there are monsters out there....

OH, YEAH! MONSTERS!

They're not taking us.

Come on, then. Let's do some sword training!

Wow!

Wow! Gee! Can I watch?

No.

I bet you'll be AWESOME!

Now let's have some fun!

This is the armory. Look around! All this will be yours soon.

Really? My goodness.

But first... I have something to give you.

The Sword of Rin — Warrior Prince and Keeper of the Forgotten Shrine.

Doesn't he want it?

No. He doesn't want it anymore.

A long time ago, it was given to me, and with it I have cut down many nightmares. Now the time has come to hand it to my successor.

That's you. Take it, already.

touch

The monkey looks nice.

Hm. She didn't look scared—that's for sure.

I'm scared all the time.

That monkey is made for the job. Why didn't they make me as well as they made her?

Oh, they didn't make you—they just raised you.

Who made me then?

Um... someone's grandma.

Great.

Hi! My name's Amali. How are you guys doing?

Fine.   Hi, Amali!

Isn't this great? I had so much fun taming beasts!

Glad to hear it.

Great dream, isn't it? I love it. Everyone's made of HAIR!

40

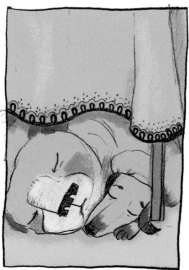

I should tell the masters.

I don't think it's for us.

Gee, check it out....

PLEASE HELP ME.
I ALWAYS HAVE THIS DREAM AND IT WON'T GO AWAY.
I AM SWIMMING IN THE SEA. IT GOES ON FOR EVER.
I SEE AN ISLAND.
THEN I SEE THAT IT'S THE TOP OF A VERY TALL TOWER AND I KNOW THE WORLD IS SUNK
AND I BECOME SINKY.
THEN I SINK DOWN AND THE WATER IS COLD AND DARK.

I DON'T WANT TO DREAM THAT ANYMORE. PLEASE MAKE IT STOP.   REGARDS, TIMMY

We're going to see the sea!

Whassgoingon?

The youngsters want to do the next mission by themselves.

Awwgreat. S'yulater.

Wait, what?

Er...

So. What's the dream?

Um...it's about the sea....

Moonfish! Wonderful.

We can't do a whole dream without you!

No problem. We will observe you.

And you'll be with me!

See you later!

Did they give you that thing? Do you know how it works?

Mm.

One ball points to where the dreamer is, and the other points back to the house. And this "whirr" is the dream pressure.

There's the tower!

Timmy! HEY! WHERE ARE YOU?

The dream pressure is going up! Swim faster!

OH, NO! OH, NO!

What?

We are TOO LATE!

He's underwater! NOOOOOOOOO!

It's OK. Looks like he's still asleep.

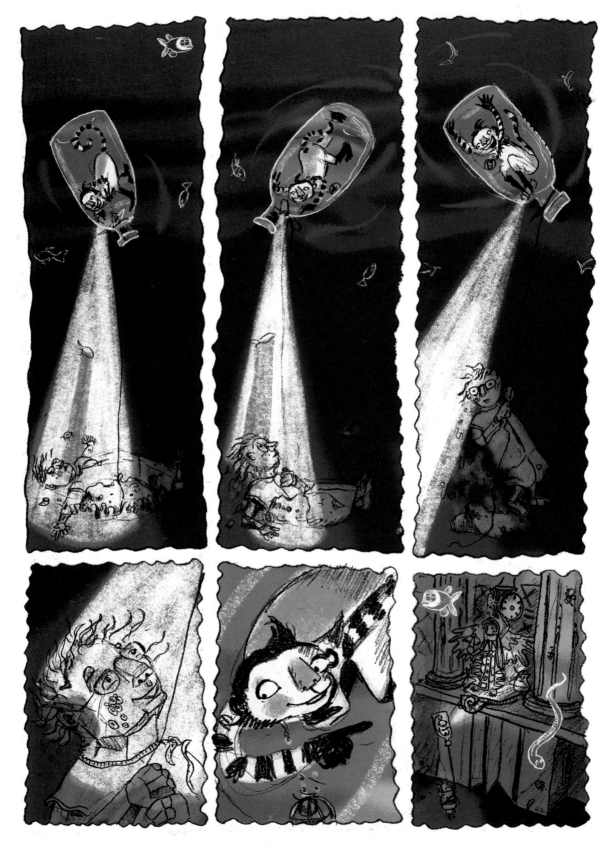

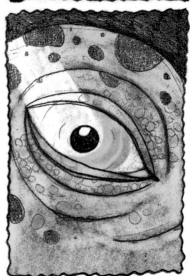

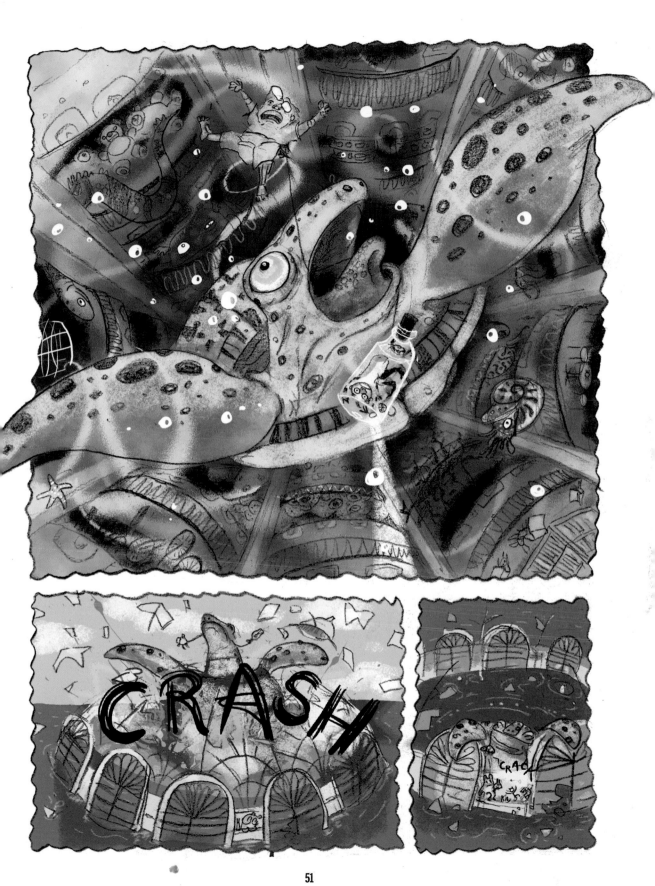

What's up?

I thought you said only you can go through that door.

Only I can come back.

Amazing creature! I believe its shell is completely horror-proof.

Can we convert it into an armored vehicle? We should ask...

Oh...

Timmy, how about a cup of tea before you leave, hm?

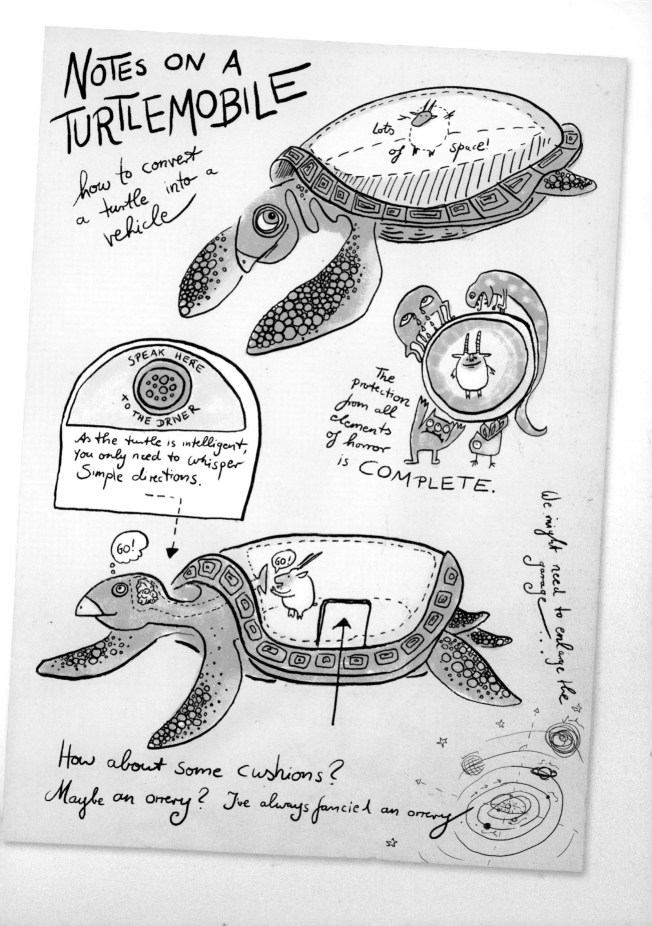

Bonno?

Yes?

I'm still sad.

If I keep being sad, I will have been happy only one day of my life.

Not necessarily. Yesterday was only sad in the afternoon. So you've had one and a half happy days out of two. At that rate, you'll be mostly happy.

True. You know more than me.

What's it like to be older?

From what I can tell, it's mostly terrifying. So far I've been frightened every day of my life.

Wow.

58

Yay! Hello!

So... usually there's a letter?

Indeed...it's just a standard N.I.P. You can handle that.

Off you go!

A standard what?

Sounds like they're having fun....

I know this smell. This is... This is school.

The child is in here....

So what's an N.I.P.?

"Naked in Public."

I DON'T WANT ANYONE TO LEAVE ANYMORE!

You're not leaving, right?

Noo. Don't worry. Not until you're ready to take over the house.

That'll be a while yet, then.

Where does that door go, anyway?

Out of dreams. Everyone has to wake up sometime. We have been dreaming for a long time....

Would you like a cup of tea?

Always!

DumDeeDoo...Mm...

The dressing up was good though, wasn't it?

Yes, the dressing up was very good.

So, it's: find the child and help. Anything else?

SLURP

Hm?

Anything else?

Nothing.

Great! Let's go!

It's dark out here.

We'd better take a flashlight!

WELCOME

You can go home now. Through that door. Then you'll wake up.

And if you dream of darkness again...um... I...I don't know.

It's OK. Thanks for saving me.

Don't worry.

She'll be back.

CLICK

73

Hello, guys.

What happened to your arm?

Ah? Oh. I must have lost it.

Fancy that.... Oh, no!

I was holding the sword on that side! Bother.

I shouldn't have brought the sword. It's yours.

Did you kill the darkness?

Of course not.

I'm sorry we messed up.

You didn't. You saved the child.

But you are hurt, and we didn't even make the nightmare go away....

Some dreams are scary every time. There is nothing you can do— except wake up.

Now you know everything. Oof.

Where are you going? You need some rest. Sit down....

I do. I need some rest. I would have liked to stick around a bit longer to see what you get up to.

I like you. We chose well.

Sorry I lost your sword, Bonno.

Can you hear that? I think it's a cat. It sounds happy. There are happy things out there. Good.

There's nothing! You are imagining it.

No, no. Time to wake up! Have a good time. Good-bye!

GOOD-BYE

GOOD-BYE

I'm just checking that you're OK.

What's wrong with Sophia?

She's run out of ink.

Hmmm, let's see.

Here you go. You got pretty worried, hm?

Buddy? What would happen to me if I went through that door?

You would wake up and be a blanket again.

You can all leave if you want.

The house can travel without you. But it would become what it once was, too. Before the Sheep captured and tamed it.

The dream of an empty home.

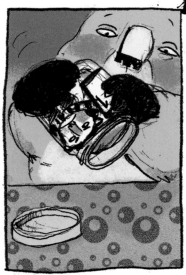

Eeeeeeeek!

I TOLD YOU TO BE QUIET!

Don't cry....

He's the one who needs to shut up....

SILENCE!

Oh...what are we supposed to do? I don't know... I...can't...

I WILL SHUT YOU UP!

Well, I'm not scared...

...any more...

...than usual.

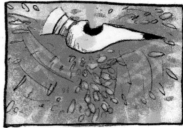

Good-bye!

Sweet dreams!

Hey, let's have breakfast again.

Can I have Chocolate Crunchies? With quadruple chocolate?

Well, as long as you can imagine what chocolate crunchies are like.

I can.

Then you can.

I'd really like a cup of tea, myself.

TOY RATTLES OR CONTAINERS - USE UNKNOWN - EARLY DYNAST

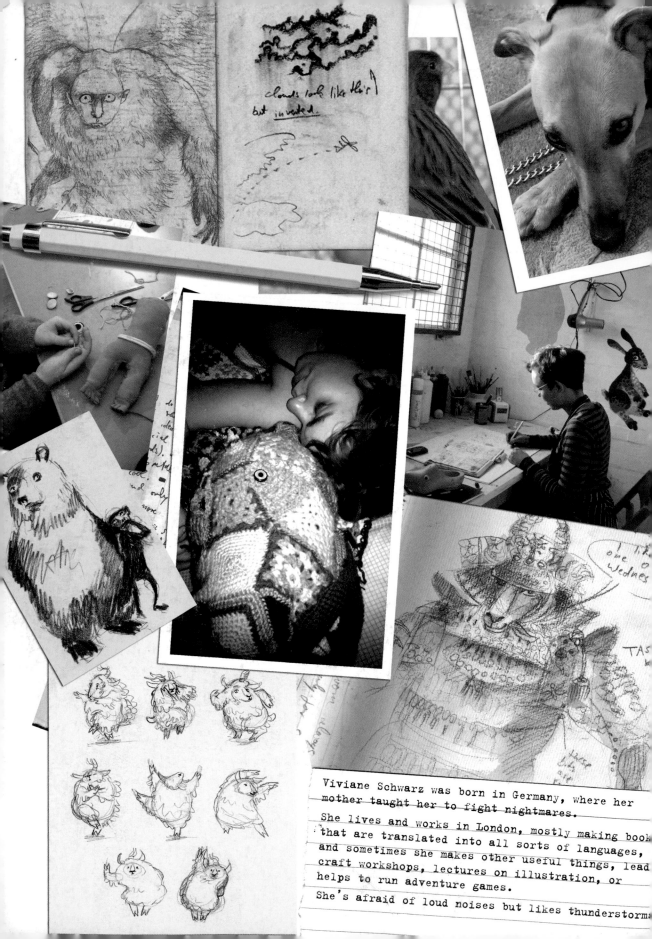

Viviane Schwarz was born in Germany, where her
mother taught her to fight nightmares.

She lives and works in London, mostly making book
that are translated into all sorts of languages,
and sometimes she makes other useful things, lead
craft workshops, lectures on illustration, or
helps to run adventure games.

She's afraid of loud noises but likes thunderstorm